Conwy Castle and Town Walls

Jeremy A. Ashbee MA, PhD, FSA

Introduction

From the road, in many parts, are most august views of the vast expanse of the river, and the majestic towers of Conwy. Similar views, and old fortified towns, I have seen frequent on the Rhine, but in magnificence far inferior to these, our British glory.

Thomas Pennant, *A Tour in Wales*, Volume 2, 1783

Opposite: Conwy Castle from across the river Conwy. Its size, grandeur and excellent state of preservation make it exceptional amongst the castles commissioned by King Edward I (1272–1307) in north Wales.

The castles of King Edward I (1272–1307) in north Wales are without doubt amongst the finest medieval buildings in Britain. Unlike the great medieval cathedrals at Durham and Canterbury, for example, Flint, Rhuddlan, Aberystwyth, Builth, Conwy, Harlech, Caernarfon and Beaumaris were all built from scratch by a single organization — the king's works — often concurrently in the uneasy aftermath of war.

Conwy is exceptional not only for the grandeur of its high towers and curtain walls, but also for its excellent state of preservation. Inside the imposing outer shell, the castle contains the most intact set of residential buildings left by the medieval English monarchy in Wales or England. With an outer ward containing a great hall, chambers and kitchen, and a more secluded inner ward with private chambers and a royal chapel, it is very easy to imagine how Conwy would have functioned when the royal entourage took up residence there. But the ambitious plans of Edward I, his designers and builders did not stop with the castle. An important monastery standing near by was moved to a site 8 miles (13km) away and around its old church the king established a new planned town for incoming settlers, ringed by a high stone wall with three twin-towered gates and twenty-one towers. Like the castle, the architectural unity and state of

preservation of the town walls are without equal. This double achievement is all the more impressive for having been raised in four short building seasons (April to November) between 1283 and 1287. The mobilization of money and men to complete this major constructional project remains staggeringly impressive.

Conwy was originally intended as a centre of administration for the local area. Although it was Caernarfon that became the shire town, Conwy nevertheless played an important role in national affairs on more than one occasion. The castle sheltered Edward I over the Christmas and spring of 1294–95, during a Welsh rebellion, and in 1399, it hosted tense negotiations between Richard II (1377–99) and his eventual captors. In 1401 it was captured by supporters of Owain Glyn Dŵr and in 1646 it was among the last strongholds to capitulate to parliament at the end of the Civil War. Although the castle had largely become redundant by this time, and was deliberately ruined soon after, it came to be appreciated for its scenic beauty and historical associations by artists, writers and eventually tourists. Since 1953, the castle and town walls have been vested in the care of the State and in 1986, as one of the 'Castles and Town Walls of King Edward in Gwynedd,' it was added to the list of World Heritage Sites.

Edward I originally intended that Conwy should be the administrative centre of a new county. In the event, Caernarfon assumed this role. This late thirteenth-century manuscript illustration depicts the king (The National Archives: PRO, E 368/69).

A History of Conwy Castle

Before the Castle

On the surface, the origins of Conwy are very simple. The castle was established on a new site in the spring of 1283, as part of a ring of new English fortresses encircling the Welsh heartland of Snowdonia in Gwynedd. Its construction can be attributed directly to the wishes of the king of England, Edward I, newly victorious in his second campaign to subdue the prince of Wales, Llywelyn ap Gruffudd (d.1282). Although these statements are true enough, the conflict that led to Edward's conquest of Wales had begun long before his accession, arising out of a long-standing dispute between the Plantagenet kings of England, John (1199–1216) and Henry III (1216–72), and the princes of Gwynedd, notably Llywelyn ab Iorwerth (d. 1240). The area in which the new castle came to be built had already played an important part in these events.

Llywelyn ab Iorwerth, also known as Llywelyn Fawr — 'the Great' — had come to enjoy considerable power over much of Wales. Although related to John through his marriage to the king's illegitimate daughter, Joan, relations with the English monarch were at best strained and at worst broke out into open warfare. Yet ultimately neither John nor his successor, Henry III, challenged the prince of Gwynedd successfully. Llywelyn maintained a castle at Degannwy (first established by the Normans in the eleventh century), set on two rocky outcrops on the eastern bank of the river Conwy. Traces of masonry and earthworks can still be seen there today. After Llywelyn's death in 1240, Henry III was quick to exploit dissent between his sons,

Gruffudd (d. 1244), who was illegitimate, and Dafydd (d. 1246), who had been proclaimed sole heir. With Gruffudd imprisoned in Criccieth Castle, Dafydd sought to strengthen his own position. But when Henry III invaded north Wales in 1241 and supported Gruffudd's cause, Dafydd was forced to surrender his prisoner to captivity in England, from which he never returned. During this episode, Degannwy Castle was severely damaged on Dafydd's orders before it could be captured by the English. In 1245, Henry III again mounted an invasion to force Dafydd's submission, during which the Cistercian abbey at Aberconwy was pillaged. Dafydd died in 1246 and in the aftermath of the conflict Henry III rebuilt Degannwy Castle as one of the most powerful royal strongholds in Wales. A town, with its own charter, was also established below the castle — a forerunner of what was to happen on the opposite bank of the river. The fortunes of the Welsh were at a low ebb, but with the emergence of a powerful new prince of Gwynedd, Llywelyn ap Gruffudd,

Opposite: Although King Edward I established Conwy in 1283, he is known to have stayed at the finished castle only once. It was towards the end of this sojourn, in February 1295, that the king met with the newly elected archbishop of Canterbury at Conwy. This late thirteenth-century manuscript illustration shows the king with a group of clergy led by an archbishop (British Library, Cotton Vitellius, Ms. A XIII, f. 6v).

Left: The Welsh prince, Llywelyn ab Iorwerth (d. 1240), held considerable power over much of Wales at the beginning of the thirteenth century. He built a series of castles in and around Snowdonia, and maintained a fortress at Degannwy on the eastern side of the river Conwy, opposite where Edward I would establish his new town and castle. This fine carved stone head — which may represent Prince Llywelyn — was found at Degannwy Castle (National Museum of Wales).

Above: The twin peaks of Degannwy Castle are clearly visible from Conwy. Little remains of the castle, which was deliberately destroyed on the orders of Prince Llywelyn ap Gruffudd following its capture by the Welsh in 1263.

Below: The arms of Llywelyn ap Gruffudd (Society of Antiquaries, London, Ms. 664, vol. iii, number 30).

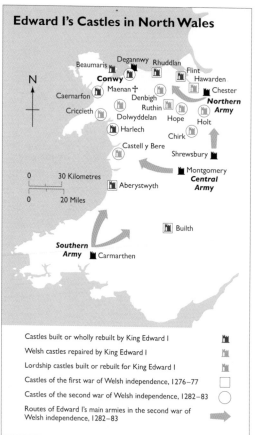

Edward I's Castles in North Wales

Castles built or wholly rebuilt by King Edward I

Welsh castles repaired by King Edward I

Lordship castles built or rebuilt for King Edward I

Castles of the first war of Welsh independence, 1276–77

Castles of the second war of Welsh independence, 1282–83

Routes of Edward I's main armies in the second war of Welsh independence, 1282–83

grandson of Llywelyn ab Iorwerth, Degannwy was again under threat. Determined to repel the English, the Welsh eventually starved the garrison at Degannwy into surrender in 1263 and on Llywelyn's orders the castle was finally destroyed. Four years later, Henry III officially recognized Llywelyn as prince of Wales.

After the accession of Edward I in 1272, relations with Llywelyn soon turned acrimonious again. The Welsh prince's refusal to do homage to the English king culminated in the war of 1276–77, in which Edward's victory was rapid if ultimately inconclusive. Faced with concerted land attacks from Chester, Montgomery and Carmarthen and against Anglesey by ship, Llywelyn was forced to agree a peace settlement with Edward I's emissaries at Aberconwy Abbey in November 1277. Besides accepting a huge fine, he conceded the lands east of the river Conwy to the English, and was left only with Snowdonia and Anglesey. Edward I sealed his success with a campaign of castle building at Builth, Aberystwyth, Rhuddlan and Flint.

The War of 1282–83

Edward's second campaign, of 1282–83, proved more decisive. Resentment at the imposition of English law in Welsh matters and the high-handed behaviour of royal officials led to outbreaks of violence in the spring of 1282, notably a surprise attack against the English garrison at Hawarden Castle by Llywelyn's treacherous younger brother, Dafydd ap Gruffudd (d. 1283). Faced with the difficult choice of fealty to the English Crown or loyalty to his brother and his people, Llywelyn sided with Dafydd, a move that led to national revolt. To this, Edward I's response was as determined as before and, even more than in the war of 1277, the king employed an overwhelming force, with an estimated 700 or 800 cavalry and over 8,000 foot soldiers in his army at any one time. In the autumn of 1282, English progress was slow and suffered numerous setbacks, but in December they won a major success when Llywelyn was killed in a skirmish near Builth. The capture of Aberconwy came in the spring of 1283, made possible by the submission of the Welsh garrison of Dolwyddelan Castle by 15 January, which gave the English control of the Conwy valley. This allowed the royal party to move along the coast to Aberconwy on the western bank of the river, where Edward I established himself on 13 March. For the time being, this was to be his command centre for military operations against Dafydd, still at large in Snowdonia. Surviving accounts show that from these earliest days, Edward planned the construction of a new castle and town to be built as a single operation. The new town was to take its name from the abbey of Aberconwy; the castle, however, was known as Conwy from the outset.

Edward stayed at Aberconwy until 9 May, probably occupying one of the buildings formerly belonging to Llywelyn, close to the Cistercian abbey in which Llywelyn ab Iorwerth and his sons were buried. The abbey itself was pressed into service, mostly as a temporary place of secure storage for the royal wardrobe (see p. 63), while more permanent buildings were being prepared to the south. Clearly, the decision to build a new castle on the high rock facing the river was taken almost immediately: as little as three or four days after Edward's arrival, woodcutters, diggers and tools were being sought to excavate the rock-cut ditch around the castle. However, as early as May, an account also mentioned 'a stockade to enclose the town of Aberconwy', the first explicit reference to an urban settlement in the vicinity. The other significant change conceived and discussed in these first weeks was the removal of the monks to a new site at Maenan, 8 miles (13 km) up the Conwy valley on the eastern bank of the river. By September, the General Chapter of the Cistercian order had granted consent for this move, and the king's master mason, James of St George, was sent to Maenan to arrange the transfer of the site to the monks. The new abbey was apparently ready for occupation within a year.

Above: Such was the strength of Welsh resistance that King Edward I was forced to mobilize a massive army in his second Welsh campaign in 1282–83. This fourteenth-century manuscript illustration shows an English king leading his troops into battle (British Library, Cotton Claudius Ms. D II, f. 33).

The parish church of St Mary, in the centre of Conwy, marks the site of the abbey of Aberconwy. King Edward arranged for the abbey to be moved 8 miles (13km) up the Conwy valley to Maenan to make space for his new town. The church is believed to incorporate some of the original stonework of the abbey church.

Above: The Welsh princes had for many years held the Croes Naid, *an important relic of the True Cross. It was presented to Edward in the summer of 1283. This depiction of the* Croes Naid *can be seen at St George's Chapel, Windsor Castle (By permission of the Dean and Canons of Windsor).*

During the summer of 1283, Edward gained a major symbolic victory at Aberconwy when a group of Welshmen presented him with the *Croes Naid*, an important relic of the True Cross, which had long been held by the princes of Wales. This preceded the king's effective triumph on 22 June 1283 when the fugitive Prince Dafydd was captured. He was later condemned to be drawn, hanged, disembowelled and quartered, with his head displayed beside Llywelyn's on the battlements of the Tower of London.

In the Statute of Wales, issued at Rhuddlan on 19 March 1284, the north Wales territories conquered in the war of 1282–83 were divided into three new counties: Anglesey, Merioneth and Caernarfon. Each was to be administered by a sheriff, under the authority of the justiciar

of north Wales, effectively the king's chief minister in the region. He was to be based in Caernarfon, where a new castle and town were likewise under construction. However, a preliminary draft suggests that this was not Edward's original wish. When works on the new castle and town began, the intention had been that Aberconwy should itself be the administrative centre of a new county.

The Construction of the Castle

The progress of the building work on the castle and town walls is comparatively well documented in contemporary royal accounts, though several gaps in the records remain. The records moreover identify by name many of the key individuals involved in the building project, notably Sir John de Bonvillars (d. 1287), later constable of Harlech Castle, who held overall authority for the works, and James of St George (d. about 1308), mason and engineer, sometimes described as 'master of the king's works in Wales'. Such entries attest to a significant presence in the administration and labour force, often in very senior roles, of foreigners recruited by Edward I from the territories of his kinsman, Count Philip of Savoy (d. 1285) — now parts of modern France, Italy and Switzerland. Also of Savoyard origin were Otto de Grandson (d. 1328), Edward I's most trusted friend and later justiciar of north Wales, William de Cicon (d. 1310/11), who in October 1284 was appointed the first constable of Conwy Castle, and the master mason, John Francis. Other important figures mentioned in the accounts were English, including the carpenter, Henry of Oxford, and Richard of Chester, 'the Engineer', cited in connection with both landscaping and building works.

Taken together, the accounts and the surviving masonry show that the buildings were raised at astonishing speed using labour drawn from almost every part of England. During late 1283 and 1284, the towers and curtain walls of

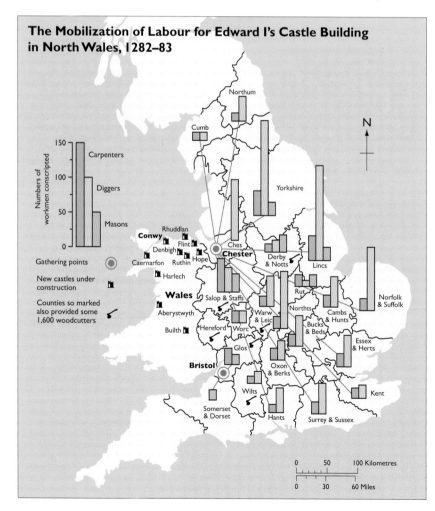

The Mobilization of Labour for Edward I's Castle Building in North Wales, 1282–83

Numbers of workmen conscripted

150
100
50
0

Carpenters
Diggers
Masons

N

Gathering points

New castles under construction

Counties so marked also provided some 1,600 woodcutters

Northum
Cumb
Yorkshire
Rhuddlan
Conwy
Flint
Denbigh
Caernarfon   Ruthin
Hope
Chester   Ches
Derby & Notts
Lincs
Harlech
Wales
Salop & Staffs
Rut
Norfolk & Suffolk
Aberystwyth
Warw & Leic
Northts
Cambs & Hunts
Builth
Hereford
Worc
Bucks & Beds
Essex & Herts
Glos
Bristol
Oxon & Berks
Kent
Wilts
Somerset & Dorset
Hants
Surrey & Sussex

0   50   100 Kilometres
0   30   60 Miles

the castle were raised as a matter of priority to establish a defensible outer shell and by November 1284, £5,800 had been spent, a massive sum equivalent to perhaps £15–£18 million today. Only a month previously, Edward had appointed the first constable, with orders to retain a garrison of thirty men. By the autumn of the following year, the curtain walls were clearly standing to their full height. Only when they were thus advanced did work begin on the buildings within the castle itself, including the hall and chambers for the king and queen. During 1285, the stone defences of the town were also under way, starting with the most vulnerable landward sections along the northern and western sides. In 1286, as the works to the castle were coming to an end, a second section of the town wall was also nearing completion. The wall running along the southern flank, containing a gate to the Gyffin watermill, was finished and connected to the first work at the south-west corner of the town by the end of September.

Unfortunately, no detailed documentation survives for late 1286 or 1287, but these years must have witnessed the effective completion of the works, with the construction of the eastern town wall along the bank of the river Conwy. The total cost of the castle and town walls amounted to around £15,000, equivalent perhaps to £45 million today.

Edward I is known to have stayed only once at his completed castle, and then in less than

Above: Conwy Castle was effectively complete by 1287 just four years after construction began. This artist's impression shows how the castle is perfectly tailored to the rocky outcrop on which it sits, surrounded on three sides by water. The inner ward with its royal apartments can be seen to the left; the outer ward with its curving great hall range is to the right (Illustration by Terry Ball, 1997).

Above left: Rapid progress was made at Conwy during 1283 and 1284, when the towers and curtain walls of the castle were built as a matter of priority. This thirteenth-century manuscript illustration shows stonemasons and carpenters at work (Trinity College Library, Ms. 177, f. 60r – The Board of Trinity College, Dublin).

Despite the provision of an impressive suite of royal apartments, King Edward is known to have stayed at the finished castle only once, over Christmas 1294 and into the spring of 1295. It was in February 1295 that the newly elected archbishop of Canterbury, Robert Winchelsey (d. 1313), arrived at Conwy to seek the king's confirmation of his appointment. This imaginative illustration depicts a meeting between the king and archbishop in the inner ward of the castle (Illustration by Peter Visscher, 2007).

ideal circumstances. In December 1294 and January 1295, while attempting to quash the rebellion of Madog ap Llywelyn (d. 1295) — a distant relative of the Gwynedd princes — Edward found himself cut off from the mass of his forces by floods and was forced to spend Christmas in Conwy Castle. The chronicler, Walter of Guisborough, describes a compellingly miserable — if slightly implausible — scene, with only a single barrel of wine left for the whole garrison. 'They were saving this for the king, but he refused it, saying "In hardship, everything must be held in common, all of us must have exactly the same. As God on high watches over us all, I am the start and cause of all this, and I should do

no better than you." Immediately afterward, Almighty God came to their aid: the floods abated, the whole army crossed to the king, and all of them now put the Welsh to flight.' On 2 February 1295, it was to Conwy that the newly elected archbishop of Canterbury, Robert Winchelsey (d. 1313), came through stormy weather to seek the king's confirmation of that office after his consecration by the pope; the castle was clearly deemed suitable for such an important meeting. Likewise in April and May 1301, the future Edward II (1307–27) stayed in Conwy, rather than at his birthplace, the still-unfinished castle at Caernarfon, to receive homage as prince of Wales.

The Fourteenth Century

During the reign of Edward II, the fortunes of Conwy Castle went into a steep decline. By the time of a survey in 1321, Conwy, like other royal castles in north and south Wales, was defective in many regards. The timbers and lead roofs of its buildings were giving particular concern, which experience would show to be a perennial shortcoming, but potentially even more alarming was the state of its armoury. Most items were in poor condition: only ten out of thirty crossbows were usable, and all of the twenty-one bows listed were without bowstrings. Most of the stores of grain, wine and the contents of the larder were also rotten.

In the early 1330s, it was reported that none of the king's castles in north Wales would be habitable if Edward III (1327–77) should go there. Although some repairs did take place, little improvement was recorded in a second survey of August 1343. In this year, the royal clerk, Sir William of Embleton, was commissioned to arrange the transfer of royal possessions in Wales to Edward, prince of Wales, later known as the Black Prince (d. 1376). Once again, Conwy Castle contained quantities of rotting and useless ammunition, made for weapons either missing or unserviceable, together with rusted mail coats and odd pieces of decaying plate armour. The great hall and its service buildings, two drawbridges, the granary, a stable and a total of eighteen rooms within six towers were 'weak and ruinous', and a 'tower outside the postern of the said castle, on which the security of the castle greatly depends' had been left unfinished. The implication is that the English were lucky that Conwy (like the other castles in north Wales) was unchallenged during this period: it could not have been defended for long.

Under the Black Prince, some attempts were made to bring the castle's buildings back to an acceptable condition. The prince's chamberlain of north Wales, Sir John of Weston, ordered repairs in 1346–47, especially to the great hall range in the outer ward, which were carried out by the prince's mason, Henry of Snelston. Entries in the Black Prince's register refer to the arches made of sandstone brought from Chester by boat, of which only one survives in the great hall range: these were evidently needed to replace the failing timber roof structure of the original thirteenth-century building. Though the documents only mention the hall, this repair programme must have encompassed or been extended to the royal apartments in the inner ward, where the remains of similar arches can also be seen (pp. 36, 41).

The survival of documents from the late fourteenth century is poor; nevertheless, there are hints that by the 1390s the castle had been

Left: By the fourteenth century, Conwy had fallen into disrepair. In 1343, when Edward, prince of Wales (1343–76), the Black Prince, received the Crown lands in the principality, a survey of the condition of the castle was conducted. This revealed that there were serious problems with the roofs and modifications were made in 1346–47. These included inserting eight stone arches in the great hall range, two of which appear in this watercolour by Thomas Girtin (d. 1802); one has since collapsed (© Trustees of the British Museum).

Below: This gilt-bronze effigy of the Black Prince rests in Canterbury Cathedral (TopFoto/ Woodmansterne).

Above: The momentous events of 1399 leading to the capture, abdication and death of Richard II (1377–99) were recorded by the chronicler, Jean Creton. This early fifteenth-century manuscript illustration depicts the fugitive king taking refuge at Conwy (British Library, Harley Ms. 1319, f. 37v).

The arms of Owain Glyn Dŵr appear on this harness decoration found at Harlech Castle (National Museum of Wales).

allowed to lapse into decay again, with 'various defects' being present. Despite the defects, more than once during August 1399, necessity led Richard II (1377–99) and courtiers loyal to him to seek refuge at Conwy from the forces of Henry Bolingbroke, the exiled duke of Lancaster, afterwards Henry IV (1399–1413). The chronicler, Jean Creton, an eyewitness to events in the royal party, later described several scenes of the increasingly harried Richard in the castle, most vividly an embassy to the king from the aged earl of Northumberland, Bolingbroke's loyal supporter. Almost certainly in the chapel in the inner ward, Northumberland took an oath in the king's presence, swearing on the consecrated Host that he and Bolingbroke meant no harm to the king. Creton concluded 'alas, his blood must have run cold at it, for he knew well to the contrary', and two days later, having tricked him into leaving the castle, Northumberland handed the king to his enemies in whose captivity he was later to die at Pontefract Castle.

The Rebellion of 1401

If the events at Conwy were calamitous for Richard II, the first years of his successor, Henry IV, saw disaster for the castle and the town. In September 1400, the first seeds of rebellion were sown when Owain Glyn Dŵr was proclaimed prince of Wales. Ostensibly caused by a boundary dispute, the rebellion was based on long-held grievances against English rule and the desire for an independent Welsh principality. After five days of insurgency a firm and rapid response by the English king appeared to have nipped the revolt in the bud. But although many Welshmen were pardoned, a series of statutes and decrees issued against the Welsh in March 1401 led to further unrest. Then, in an apparently isolated and daring incident on Good Friday (1 April) 1401, when the garrison of Conwy was at prayer, two of the unpardoned rebels and cousins of Glyn Dŵr, Gwilym and Rhys ap Tudur, took the castle 'through the guile of a carpenter claiming to be about his usual job, who killed the two watchmen'.

The brothers and their adherents held the castle against the English for around three months, but eventually negotiated its surrender having at last secured their pardons, partly at the expense of some of their own comrades. The delay in reaching a settlement had been caused by disagreement among the English about what terms to allow, largely because the Welsh rebels had sacked the town. The townspeople of Conwy (still overwhelmingly with English names) later petitioned the prince of Wales, the future Henry V (1413–22), for compensation making two particularly eloquent, if suspiciously extravagant, claims:

'Item, the said rebels completely burnt down all the houses in the town of Conwy together with the bridges, gates, exchequer and the dwellings of the justiciar and chamberlain there, causing damages to our lord prince and the burgesses of the said town at £5,000.'

'Item, the same rebels took all the records then in the exchequer of our lord prince there and the said lord's account rolls, the hundred and court rolls of the sheriff, witness papers and parcels of bills for the repairs of Conwy Castle, with various other indentures and muniments, a damage to our lord prince of £10,000.'

The loss of the records, though grievous to the historian, is most unlikely to have cost twice as much as the burning of the town and its buildings. The Welsh rebels' capture of Conwy, though short-lived, proved a rallying cry to their compatriots to join a revived widespread insurgency under Glyn Dŵr's leadership during the next few years.

The garrison of the castle was reinforced during the most unsettled years of the War of the Roses (1455–85), between the houses of Lancaster and York; otherwise little is recorded about its fortunes.

The Tudors and Stuarts

For much of the fifteenth century and the first years of the sixteenth, detailed information about the castle is lacking. However, in the 1520s and 30s during the reign of the second Tudor king, Henry VIII (1509–47), the castle and town walls were substantially repaired. The accounts make it clear that the castle was then used as an armament store and prison for petty felons and debtors. However, payments for repair and redecoration of the former royal apartments in the inner ward and the 'Prince's Hall' in the outer ward suggest that some kind of residential or administrative use was planned. Perhaps Henry intended that a future prince of Wales should stay here, or his illegitimate son, the duke of Richmond (d.1536), or, more likely, the Council of the Marches, which visited Conwy in 1541.

Despite the efforts spent in maintaining the castle at this time, Conwy lay far from the centre of political power, and with monarchs of Welsh descent on the throne, the need for the huge castles of north Wales became less and less apparent. Indeed, in 1586, the antiquarian

The Glyn Dŵr rebellion was revived in April 1401 when a daredevil raid succeeded in capturing Conwy Castle and sacking the town. This aerial view shows the full extent of the medieval borough.

Left: A detail from the 1534 maintenance accounts recording repair works to the Prison Tower at Conwy Castle (The National Archives, PRO E 101/489/9).

Major General Thomas Mytton (d. 1656) commanded the parliamentary forces that besieged Conwy in 1646. This portrait appears in John Vicar's England's Worthies..., *published in London in 1647 (British Library).*

Disenchanted with his fellow royalists, Williams now turned to the parliamentarians, who had previously mocked the spectacle of an armoured archbishop in their pamphlets. In August 1646, it was with information from Williams that the parliamentarian commander, Major General Thomas Mytton (d.1656), attacked Conwy. The town was soon taken, but the castle held out until November, even after Charles I had permitted its garrison to surrender. Conwy was one of the last three castles in the country to be taken.

Slighting and Dismantling

Although hostilities had ceased, it was decided that Conwy Castle should remain operational, and it was essential that damage inflicted in the siege be repaired by the parliamentarian governor, Colonel John Carter. The castle was still potentially useful as an emplacement for artillery, and as a place of security for prisoners. However, this resolution was short lived. In 1655, the Council of State ordered that Conwy should be 'slighted', or made indefensible, a fate that befell many other fortresses. It seems most likely that the enormous hole in the masonry of the Bakehouse Tower was made at this time; later tradition suggested, probably unjustly, that this damage resulted from pilfering of stone by the local inhabitants.

The final act in the reduction of Conwy Castle to ruin came in the summer of 1665. The third Lord Conway (d. 1683), to whom the castle was returned after the restoration of the monarchy in 1660, could find no use for it. Determined to realize as much of his asset as possible, he sent his agent, William Milward, to salvage the castle's ironwork and the lead from the roofs. Milward wrote several times to his employer about the frustratingly slow progress of the works. He found great difficulty in recruiting experienced labourers, particularly for the dangerous business of removing lead from the roofs, whose rotten timber beams had never properly been maintained, even by Archbishop Williams and Colonel Carter. Eventually, he sought the help

In 1655, the Council of State ordered that Conwy Castle should be made indefensible, or slighted. It seems likely that it was at this time that stone was removed from the Bakehouse Tower, at the weakest point between the inner and outer wards of the castle. The damage done to the tower is clearly visible in this watercolour by Thomas Girtin (Ashmolean Museum, Oxford).

Artists and Antiquarians

of a man from 'Blewmarris (Beaumaris) that hath taken downe one or two castels alredye.' Those workmen Milward did find were subjected to threats of retribution for damaging what was still seen as a royal castle. The leading local inhabitants were doubtless equally offended by Milward calling the area 'a beggarly cuntrye', and on at least one occasion they threatened him with pistols. Milward complained that in addition to harassment of his labourers, pilfering of materials was widespread; he dealt with this by ordering that torches were to be burned at night inside the castle to show any would-be raiders that the site was manned. But in spite of all these setbacks, the works went on and within months, the castle's buildings were completely unroofed. Compared with many other castles, the fabric of Conwy had escaped relatively unharmed. Nevertheless, it was inescapable that its history as a habitable site had come to an end.

The ruined castle now began to exercise a fascination for travellers and artists. Antiquarians and topographers such as Francis Grose (d. 1791) and Thomas Pennant (d. 1798) wrote detailed and informative descriptions of visits to the castle. Some of the buildings had already received imaginative names such as 'Tŵr y Brenin' (the King's Tower) or 'Queen Elinor's Toilet' (the chapel in the inner ward). Celebrated artists such as Paul Sandby (d. 1809), Moses Griffith (d. 1819), Julius Caesar Ibbetson (d. 1817), Thomas Girtin (d. 1802) and J. M. W. Turner (d. 1851) recorded the appearance of the castle and town as they then were.

Several of their works are all the more evocative today because many of the most

By the late eighteenth and early nineteenth centuries, Conwy began to attract artists in search of the 'picturesque' and 'sublime'. The majestic ruins were as yet uncluttered by the intrusion of road and rail bridges as can be seen in this magnificent oil painting by J. M. W. Turner (d. 1851). Based on the artist's tours in north Wales in 1798–99, the painting was probably completed in 1802–03 (Private Collection/The Bridgeman Art Library).

Right: The arrival of the first road bridge in 1826 (centre) and the rail bridge in 1848 (right) allowed greater numbers of visitors to discover Conwy. A third bridge was added in 1958; all three can be seen from the east barbican of the castle.

A photograph of about 1868–70, in which carriages can be seen below the outer gate. The drivers are presumably awaiting the return of visitors to the castle.

prized vistas of the castle have changed since the 1820s, with the coming of new transport routes to Conwy, particularly the bridging of the river immediately east of the castle. The first of these was Thomas Telford's suspension bridge of 1826, carrying the main Chester to Bangor road across the river to run through the town. At the same time, an additional gate was driven through Tower 10 of the medieval town walls for the road to leave the town and head westwards. From 1848, Robert Stephenson's tubular bridge brought the Chester and Holyhead railway below the south wall of the castle, into the town through a new arch in the

town wall and out again via a tunnel underneath Tower 11. Since 1958, a third bridge has stood beside them carrying the modern road into the town from the direction of Llandudno.

All of these factors helped to bring more visitors to Conwy so that gradually tourism was placed on a firmer footing. In 1865, the castle passed from the possession of the Holland family — who had leased it from the marquesses of Hertford, descendants of the Conways — into the care of the mayor, bailiffs and burgesses of Conwy. Twenty years later, when the office of constable was once again united with that of the mayor (as Edward I had originally stipulated), the castle came completely under the control of the town corporation. Through the second half of the nineteenth century, some restoration works were carried out for the benefit of visitors. Parts of the town walls were restored at the expense of John Henry Parker (d. 1884), Keeper of the Ashmolean Museum, Oxford, and the Bakehouse Tower in the castle was restored at the expense of the London and North Western Railway Company. The town corporation also carried out smaller works of conservation in the castle.

The Twentieth Century

In the second half of the twentieth century, the understanding, conservation and presentation of the castle and town walls at Conwy were revolutionized through the work of Arnold J. Taylor (1911– 2002). As Inspector of Ancient Monuments (ultimately Chief Inspector) for the Ministry of Works and its successor organizations, Taylor assumed responsibility for the castle and town walls after they came into the Ministry's guardianship in 1953 on a ninety-nine-year lease from the Conway Corporation. He supervised a new programme of repairs and acquired considerable knowledge of their constructional and architectural details. He was able to combine this with exhaustive researches of the medieval documents, especially the records of the English exchequer held in the Public Record Office (now the National Archives). These allowed him to trace the careers of many of the craftsmen who built the Welsh castles, notably James of St George, master of Edward I's works in Wales.

It was Taylor who first realized that Master James, John Francis and several of their colleagues hailed from the county of Savoy (now parts of France, Italy and Switzerland). Here, castles and urban defences such as Chillon, Saillon and Yverdon still attest to their expertise in castle building before Edward I recruited them in the late 1270s. Having explored the monuments and archives of Savoy, Taylor further argued that the castles of Wales incorporated 'Savoyard' features of design and construction, such as the forms and dimensions of windows, arches, battlements and fireplaces, and the use of ramped scaffolding during building. This combination of detailed and wide-ranging documentary work with close examination of the monuments set a new standard in research of this kind that has rarely been equalled since. Taylor's work on Conwy and the other Edwardian castles of Wales still forms the core of current knowledge and exercises a marked influence on present research.

Taylor and his colleagues were equally anxious to improve the visual impact of the town walls and successfully negotiated the removal of various unsightly modern buildings, in particular those that obscured the wall along the north-west side from Tower 5 to Tower 13, which can now be seen to impressive effect. The walls themselves were conserved and long stretches of the wall-walk once again opened to the public, a scheme extended in recent years with a new section from the Upper Gate to Tower 17 opened in 2006. Moreover, in 1980, it was Taylor's vigorous opposition to a planned new road crossing of the river Conwy beside the castle that was largely responsible for the alternative scheme of a road tunnel beneath the river, which now bypasses the town centre.

In 1986 the medieval fortifications in their beautiful natural setting received due international recognition when they were designated part of the World Heritage Site of 'The Castles and Town Walls of King Edward in Gwynedd.' Conwy Castle and town walls are now cared for by Cadw, the historic environment service of the Welsh Assembly Government.

Arnold J. Taylor (1911–2002), the inspirational scholar whose diligent research did so much to help us understand the builders and building of Conwy Castle and town walls. It was Taylor's work too that ensured the clearance of many of the buildings that obscured the town walls in the 1950s and 60s (Patricia Taylor).

Below: A 1956 view along the town walls, between Towers 7 and 9 on Town Ditch Road, prior to the clearance of adjacent buildings.

A Tour of Conwy Castle

This tour suggests a route around the castle and describes the principal features of interest. It is not intended to be rigid and visitors may investigate the various parts of the castle in any order using the bird's-eye view (inside front cover) or the ground plan (inside back cover). Our route, however, begins by looking at the external features of the castle before proceeding to the outer ward. Further directions appear in the text.

The Exterior of the Castle

For sheer visual impact, even in its ruined state, Conwy Castle has few rivals among the medieval fortresses of Europe. Among the most impressive views of the castle is that seen from the top of the watchtower (Tower 13) on the town walls. From here, it appears as a dense cluster of battlemented towers standing out against the background of the river Conwy (p. 46). But for many, it is the view from across the river Conwy that defies comparison, with the castle set against the mountains of Snowdonia, ancient heartland of Welsh princes (p. 2). It is hard not to believe that those who first planned and built the castle were driven to create something visually magnificent as well as militarily strong.

The form of the castle has never been hidden from an onlooker outside its lofty walls. From most angles, especially from the north and south, it is easy to appreciate that Conwy Castle is roughly rectangular in plan, with a rank of four towers spaced regularly along each long side. The south wall contains a pronounced outwards bow, no doubt the result of the builders following the contours of the rocky outcrop

on which the castle was built. Four of the towers — those nearest the river — bear small round turrets, a feature absent elsewhere in the castle. They were built in this way because they overlook the inner ward of the castle, where the royal apartments were located. While there would be a good military reason for providing watchtowers from which sentries could guard this most sensitive part of the castle, it seems just as likely that the turrets were designed to allow the royal standard to be flown when the king or the prince of Wales was in residence at Conwy.

All around the castle's exterior, there are indications of the uses to which the rooms inside were put. Many of the openings are narrow slits — loops — which were originally protected by iron bars that made the rooms secure, but very dark [1]. The settings for these bars can still be seen in the surrounding sandstone. Other windows indicate something more comfortable. All of the towers contain at least one and usually several large rectangular windows, which

There is level access to the visitor centre. From here, there is a sloping path with steps to the castle entrance. Inside, the ground levels vary with cobbled and gravelled paths. Stone steps give access to the wall-walks and towers.

Left: The reverse of the great seal of King Edward I (The National Archives).

Opposite: The plan of Conwy Castle can be clearly appreciated in this aerial view. Essentially rectangular in shape, the castle is divided into two wards of unequal size, both of which contain four massive towers. The four towers in the foreground are distinguished by turrets, which overlook the inner ward — the most private and secure part of the castle that contained the royal apartments.

The castle's latrines discharged outside the walls. Those on the south side (A) projected out over the rocks of the Gyffin, supported on stone corbels above the precipitous drop. This example is situated next to the Prison Tower.

Below: The north-west tower displays many of the characteristic features to be seen on the exterior walls of the castle. The numbers highlight several of the features described in the text.

originally had stone mullions (vertical bars) dividing them into two parts, or lights [2]. These windows, invariably with stone window seats, helped make the rooms light and airy, and provided pleasant alcoves for their occupants to sit in and talk, or for clerks to work in daylight.

The outlets for latrines are another reminder of the practicalities of daily life; they can be seen in the curtain walls beside most of the towers. Those on the north side facing the town and the river Conwy were set low, immediately above the natural rock. These chutes were potential weak points in the castle's defences, places where a particularly determined intruder could climb into the castle. For this reason they were protected by masonry covers: one remains in place at the foot of the north-west tower [3]. On the south side, the outlets are designed differently, as stone projections at high level, corbelled out from the wall with their seats overlooking a sheer drop to the rocks of the Gyffin far below.

Other small details are also best seen from outside the castle. The round towers in particular show clear evidence of the way in which the castle was built, with diagonal lines of small square holes running upwards in a spiral pattern [4]. These 'putlog holes' indicate where the horizontal timber beams of the builders' scaffolding (the putlogs) were set in the stonework, creating ramps by which the labourers could haul their materials to the wall-top. This type of scaffolding was most unusual in England and Wales, and its appearance at Edward I's Welsh castles, including Conwy, Harlech and Beaumaris, has been interpreted as a legacy of foreign craftsmen in the labour force. Certainly, similar ramped putlog holes can be seen on numerous buildings in Savoy, the homeland of Edward I's master of works, James of St George, and several of his most important colleagues. Some of the best examples can be found at the castles of Chillon, Saillon, Saxon and La Bâtiaz (Martigny), all in modern Switzerland.

Savoyard influence has also been cited to explain another detail at Conwy, notably on the

Evidence for the use of spiral scaffolding — a Savoyard building technique — can be found in numerous locations around the castle and town walls at Conwy. In this fifteenth-century French manuscript illustration, a king and his master mason watch building progress with the use of a spiral (helicoidal) scaffolding ramp (British Library, Royal Ms. 15 D. III, f. 15v).

south-west tower. Like the fortification at San Giorio, now in Italy, the Conwy battlements were decorated with three finials on each upstanding section or merlon [5]. These finials, spikes of rough stonework, were not limited to the towers; a few traces can also be seen on sections of the curtain wall, though the battlements here are generally less well preserved. The towers of the castle (but not the intervening wall-walks) were also equipped with arrowloops in the centre of each merlon, alternating between two levels: this enabled crossbowmen on the parapet to command both the near and middle distance around the castle [6].

Several different interpretations have been proposed for the lines of square holes that appear below the battlements of the towers and wall-walks, as well as on the town walls [7].

The simplest suggestion is that they were drain outlets, very necessary in the castle, although on the steeper sections of the town walls such drains would have been superfluous. Another idea, previously favoured by scholars, is that they contained the horizontal beams for wooden fighting platforms, sometimes called brattices or hourds, projecting externally from the wall-tops. A third more picturesque interpretation, suggested by building accounts for some of Edward I's other castles, is that the holes were for logs, supporting round shields (targes) painted with the royal arms. This is inspired by a biblical image from the *Song of Songs* (chapter 4, verse 4) in the Old Testament. Although the idea of decorating the exterior of a castle may seem unacceptably frivolous to the modern mind, it was entirely characteristic of thirteenth- and fourteenth-century castle builders to

A well-preserved group of three finials on one of the merlons of the south-west tower.

One of the most startling features of medieval Conwy was the brilliant white walls of the castle. This manuscript illustration, depicting the arrival of the earl of Salisbury at Conwy during the events leading to Richard II's abdication in 1399, vividly portrays the appearance of the castle. The earl of Salisbury, John Montagu (d. 1400), was a loyal supporter of the king; his arrival via ship is a reminder of the importance of sea travel and the castle's proximity to the Conwy estuary (British Library, Harley Ms. 1319, f. 14v).

temper practical military considerations with thoughts of aesthetics and symbolism.

The same concern for appearances (and biblical imagery) also lies behind the most startling feature of the medieval castle: its walls were originally white. Evidence for this white covering (a lime render) can be seen in many places around the castle, notably at the castle's entrance (the west barbican gate and north-west tower), and also inside the castle, particularly at the eastern end of the outer ward. Although functional as a waterproofing agent, this type of decoration, known on numerous contemporary castles and most famously the White Tower of the Tower of London, would have completely altered the appearance of Conwy. Were we to imagine the castle with gleaming white walls, heraldic banners, painted window shutters and shields hanging from the battlements, the present gaunt and intimidating exterior would turn into something recognizable from an illuminated medieval manuscript.

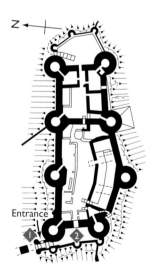

The Outer Gate ◆❶
and West Barbican ◆❷

The modern bridge across the road from the visitor centre leads to the path that winds up the slope to the outermost gate of the castle. The medieval approach from the town was much more direct. A steep ramped causeway ran up from the present Castle Street to a dry ditch in front of the castle's outer gate (see reconstruction drawing, p. 9). Only the last few feet of this masonry ramp still survive. The gap between the ramp and the gate was spanned by a pivoting wooden drawbridge, the axle for which lay slightly below the present decking in the gateway. The modern path passes under the site of the drawbridge, turns to approach the gate and leads through a rough opening broken through the side wall of the projecting gateway.

The arch of the medieval outer gate was secured with a portcullis, the slots for which can still be seen to either side of the opening. The outer gate seems to have been open to the sky and the mechanism for the portcullis may have been contained in a small hut above the arch, reached by stone stairs to either side of the entrance passage. The entrance façade was also ornamented with two small turrets, large enough for a sentry apiece, but not capable of serious defence.

The path continues upwards, past the remains of a doorway that closed the inner end of the gate-passage, into a narrow enclosure or barbican, under the shadow of the two huge towers at the western end of the castle. The barbican was an ideal place in which an attacker could be held at bay between the outer gate and the entrance to the castle proper. Even in peacetime, however, a visitor to the castle could not fail to be intimidated by the scale of the defences. Most striking was the line of 'murder holes', or machicolations, projecting beyond the parapet of the main curtain wall

between the two western towers. Supported on elaborate multi-tiered stone corbels, these allowed soldiers on the wall-walk above to drop stones or other projectiles onto anyone attacking the main gate below. The Conwy machicolations are thought to be the earliest surviving examples of such a feature in stone anywhere in Britain, and are certainly among the most ostentatious. The castle's main entrance through the west wall was itself strongly protected, with two wooden bars across the opening, then a portcullis and finally a pair of timber gates opening inward, secured by drawbars.

The barbican offers impressive views westward, across the rock-cut ditch and along the town wall, with the scenic Gyffin valley beyond: the three small turrets at regular intervals in its wall would have made ideal lookout posts.

Below top left: The outer gate to the castle. The remains of the steep masonry ramp up to the gate can be seen to the right of this view.

Below bottom left: The west barbican and gate into the outer ward were defended by an elaborate series of machicolations — 'murder holes'.

Below: A reconstruction of the machicolations in the west barbican showing the way they may have been used during an attack on the gateway leading to the outer ward (Illustration by Chris Jones-Jenkins, 1990).

A view of the outer ward looking west towards the gatehouse. The curving great hall range is to the left, with the chapel in the foreground. The site of the kitchen and later stables is to the right. The north-west (right) and south-west (left) towers at the far end would have been connected by a timber-framed building that ran across the back of the gatehouse.

The Outer Ward ◆3

This part of the tour explores the buildings in the courtyard and three of the four towers, which contain reconstructed spiral stairs. Each building and tower is described individually, and you may wish to return to the courtyard before moving on to the next building.

The outer ward is the larger of the two wards in the castle and the more accessible from the town. Though now an open courtyard, mostly laid out as a lawn, this was a much narrower space in the Middle Ages flanked by large buildings, several of which have since been lost. Despite the

slightly cramped area, the outer ward should be imagined as a hive of activity, often busy with the castle's officers, soldiers, servants and craftsmen, as well as the townspeople of Aberconwy, for whom the castle was their centre of administration. In contrast, the inner ward at the far end of the castle was intended as a more private residence for the king, the queen and the most important members of the royal household. The division of the wards at Conwy closely resembles the layout intended for Caernarfon Castle, though it was never completed there. At Conwy, however, the buildings were finished as planned and their configuration is clearer than at any medieval castle in Wales or England.

The Main Gate ◆ 4

The two towers at the western end of the castle now stand apart from each other, but, like numerous other castles of the period, they were originally linked to form a large gatehouse. A missing building, running between the towers, was still standing, though in ruinous condition in 1627, when it was described as two upper storeys above a 'low dark roome' to either side of the gate-passage. The lost building, probably in stone at ground level and timber framed above with a lead-covered roof, contained porters' lodges at ground level, and guard rooms, with the mechanism to raise and lower the portcullis on the first floor immediately over the gate. An additional entrance to this room was provided from the wall-walk above, with a stairway running down through the curtain wall to the room over the entrance passageway.

Close examination of the surviving structure indicates that the two towers of the gatehouse were designed slightly differently. Although both had two storeys of chambers over basements, it is notable that the southern tower is better provided with fireplaces and latrines. The designers of the castle almost certainly intended different functions for the two towers.

The North-West Tower ◆ 5

The north-west tower could be entered at ground level only by passing through the porters' lodge. Its basement was unheated and dimly lit by narrow slit windows (one of them later blocked); it was probably used for the castle's stores. On the two upper floors, the tower contained some concessions to comfort — fireplaces and large two-light windows with stone seats — but it possessed only one latrine situated in a small room in the thickness of the curtain wall reached from the spiral stair. The latrine was approached through a small antechamber containing a blocked-up flue or vent in its roof. The two upper chambers contain traces of wall plaster.

The South-West Tower ◆ 6

In contrast, the south-west tower had its own entrance in a small courtyard, reached by passing through the main gate and climbing the steps on the right. It may have been intended as the residence of an important figure, such as the constable of Conwy, who commanded and paid the castle's garrison. However, the courtyard that contained the tower's entrance was itself a busy thoroughfare, leading to a common latrine; likewise the latrine serving this tower's uppermost chamber could be entered from the main wall-walk, allowing little privacy. It is perhaps more likely that a section of the garrison used part or all of the south-west tower. As originally constituted in 1284, the garrison was to contain thirty soldiers, of whom fifteen had to be crossbowmen, together with a chaplain, blacksmith, carpenter, mason and an engineer to maintain the weapons. This was the same size as the complement at Harlech and ten men fewer than at Caernarfon and Castell y Bere.

The basement of the south-west tower served as a bakehouse and contains a bread oven on its eastern side. This greater emphasis on domesticity can also be seen in the upper rooms in the tower: its fireplaces are larger than

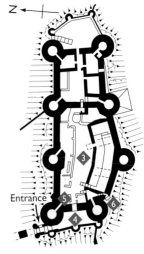

Left: A room would have occupied the space above the gate-passage. From here, the machinery to operate the portcullis would have been worked.

The basement of the south-west tower contains a large oven and suggests that this tower was more domestic in function than its northern counterpart. This early fourteenth-century manuscript illustration shows a baker at work (The Bodleian Library, University of Oxford, Ms. Douce 49, f. 9v).

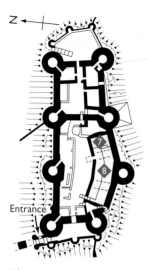

The unusual curved shape of the great hall range was determined by the nature of the site. Although it now appears as one long room, the interior was divided into at least two sections — the chapel and great hall.

those in the corresponding tower to the north. The first-floor room was additionally provided with a small lobby within the thickness of the wall, leading to a latrine. This lobby, though rather dark, lay behind the flue of the bread oven and may have been agreeably warm. The room above was also provided with access to a latrine in a stone-built hut at the level of the wall-walk.

Climbing to the top of the tower, two pieces of evidence for the form of the battlements and roof survive. Throughout the castle, there are signs that each merlon (the upstanding part of a battlement; the gap between two merlons is called a crenel or embrasure) was topped with three rough pinnacles (see p. 23). Most have lost one or more of them, but the best-preserved examples are to be seen on this tower. The wall-walk also contains an upstanding kerb with gutters running outwards. This is most likely to relate to the early roof structure of the tower,

although it is not entirely clear what form the roof would have taken. A previous suggestion that the towers were capped with high conical roofs now seems unlikely; the roofs were probably low pitched so that to an onlooker the pinnacled merlons formed the skyline.

Chapel  and Great Hall 8

A range of stone buildings runs along the southern side of the outer ward. Built against the south curtain wall, its curved plan follows that of the outer wall. The main rooms in the range lay at the level of the courtyard, lit by rectangular windows in the south curtain and by three elaborate traceried windows facing the courtyard. Underneath this level, part of the rock was quarried away to create basements, accessible from the courtyard by a stair at the western end. The main entrance to the building,

formerly covered by a timber porch, lies towards its eastern end, up three steps.

This range was originally partitioned into two or more smaller spaces and included some of the most important rooms in the castle. A document of 1343 mentions the 'king's great hall in the castle and a cellar under the said hall', and these were certainly among the rooms in this range. However, the space at the eastern end, to the left of the entrance from the courtyard, has been identified as one of the castle's two chapels. The chapel would have been flooded with light from two windows in the south wall, one of the three windows towards the courtyard, and a large and elaborate traceried window in the east wall. There was a stone altar below the east window, the base of which is just discernible within the arched recess. A timber screen or partition would have divided the chapel from the rest of the range.

The central part of the range was the great hall. The great hall of a royal castle was used for banquets and ceremonies, and would also typically host court hearings. Under the charter of the town of Aberconwy, issued by Edward I in 1284, the constable of the castle was also mayor of the town and was authorized to imprison criminals in the castle 'in cases of life and limb'. It is no coincidence that the tower leading off the great hall contained the most secure rooms in the castle, ideal for imprisonment.

It has also been suggested that there were two further partitions, dividing the remainder of the building into two more rooms. This is based on the presence of three large fireplaces, one in each of the side walls and one in the wall at the western end. It is certainly unusual (though not unknown) for a medieval room to have contained more than one fireplace and the suggested arrangement is very plausible, but any evidence for the actual partitions has been lost through later changes to the roof structure of the building. Such a compartmented plan might help to make sense of a confusing reference in 1286 to 'building... a pantry next to the small hall in the great hall'.

Above: An artist's impression of the eastern end of the great hall range as it may have appeared in the late 1280s. The chapel, at the far end, is divided from the rest of the range by a timber partition; further timber partitions suggest that the remainder of the range may have been divided into three rooms, one of which would have served as the great hall shown here in the foreground (Illustration by Terry Ball, 1998).

Left: The great hall at Conwy would have been the scene of lavish entertainment, such as that shown in this fourteenth-century French manuscript illustration, where a king and queen entertain guests at the high table (British Library, Royal Ms. 14 E III, f. 89).

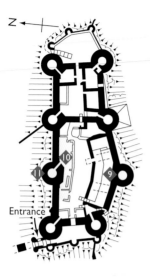

This range also contains evidence for one of the most dramatic alterations made to Conwy Castle: the reconstruction of the roof in the late 1340s. The original roofs of Edward I's buildings were covered in lead and supported on timber arched braces. Traces of several of the corbels that supported the timber trusses can still be seen in the masonry. By 1321, these roofs were in poor condition; fourteen years later the state of the leadwork and rotten timbers had become critical. The solution adopted in 1346–47 by Henry of Snelston, mason to Edward, the Black Prince — who had recently been granted the castle with the principality of Wales — was to replace the timber roof structure with a series of eight stone arches spanning the range. Only one of these arches now survives intact, in the former chapel, but projecting stubs of masonry show where the lost arches formerly sprang from the walls. The arches were dressed with Cheshire sandstone, shipped from the quarries to the castle. These reconstructed roofs survived, often in poor condition, until the seventeenth century, when the castle was finally reduced to ruin.

Prison Tower 9

On the south side of the great hall, almost opposite the entrance, is an unobtrusive doorway leading from a window reveal into the southernmost tower of the castle, known as the Prison Tower. The name is appropriate: although the two upper floors contained fairly comfortable rooms with fireplaces and windows fitted with stone window seats, the lower levels of the tower were more stark, designed with security in mind.

From the passage from the hall, a stair runs down to a doorway before turning sharp left to another doorway — the entrance to the ground-floor room. This room was different from the courtyard-level rooms in the other towers: its doorway was set some 4 feet (1.3m) above the floor level of the tower, difficult to reach without a ladder. Previous imaginative descriptions have evoked the disorientation of a prisoner thrown down unexpectedly into the darkness of the room. The door could have been sealed from outside by a wooden drawbar.

Right: The Prison Tower can be approached from the great hall through an inconspicuous doorway hidden in the right-hand side of this window reveal, which is almost opposite the main doorway from the courtyard.

Far right: A fifteenth-century manuscript illustration depicting an unfortunate prisoner in shackles (British Library, Harley Ms. 4375, f. 140).

This room is firmly identified as the 'dettors chambre' in several accounts of the 1530s, when numerous repairs were carried out to improve the prison accommodation. The partial blocking of the 'gret wyndoo' at this level, still visible, is mentioned in these accounts, which also speak of repairs to the floor, hooks and hinges for the doors and a wooden bed frame for the prisoners. The inmates can have been no worse than petty criminals.

Much more chilling, however, is the pit beneath this room, described in 1534 as 'the doungeon under the dettors towre'. More than one account speaks of the need to clean this room, which seems generally to have been filthy. The dungeon, 12 feet (3.1m) deep with sheer walls and only a tiny window high above the floor, has no door: prisoners must have been let down by rope through a trap door in the floor above. It was perhaps this trap door that received a lock in 1534, making an already forbidding prison unbreakable.

Kitchen ⑩ and Kitchen Tower ⑪

On the north side of the outer ward, opposite the great hall range, stood a series of buildings now reduced to low stone footings at ground level. These structures, built against the north curtain wall, are interpreted as service buildings. The 1343 survey of the castle included a report on 'the kitchen, brewhouse and bakehouse under one roof', stating that this roof was already ruinous and would need £60 to repair it. This item, coming between similarly damning accounts of the king's great hall and the drawbridge connecting the outer and inner wards, almost certainly refers to these buildings. The household ordinances of Edward I, written in 1279, only four years before the construction of Conwy Castle, stipulated that there should exist two kitchen organizations, one to serve the king himself and the other comprising 'the cooks of the kitchen of the household': the latter must have been based in one of these

rooms. A more private kitchen was located in the royal apartments.

Little more is said about these buildings in the castle's accounts. The kitchen was evidently still standing in 1535–36, when Arthur Sclater was paid for covering its roof with 100 slates. In 1627, surveyors found that this roof (now lead covered) had collapsed and was lying on the ground. One room in the eastern part contained an old manger and had apparently been converted into a stable. The

An artist's impression showing a cutaway view of the Prison Tower as it may have appeared in the mid-fourteenth century (Illustration by Chris Jones-Jenkins, 2005).

A wide ditch was cut from north to south across the castle rock to separate the inner and outer wards. The castle well was dug at the centre of this ditch and beyond it lay a drawbridge and the small, projecting middle gate.

Two of the triangular coping stones, which may have come from a crenellated parapet to the great hall range, now reset in the modern path.

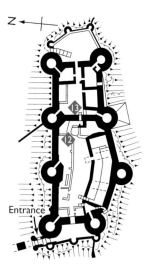

positions of the walls dividing one building from the next can still be traced, but beyond this little can be seen today and it is not possible to see where hearths or bread ovens once stood, nor the trough that was ordered to be excavated in the 'hall's kitchen' in 1307–08.

The only ground-level door into the adjacent tower in the north curtain wall lay inside this range. The function of the tower must have been closely connected to that of the building, hence the name, Kitchen Tower. This tower contains an unheated basement, perhaps a larder or some other storeroom, with two chambers above. Both of these upper rooms have large and well-preserved fireplaces. However, the spiral stair has not been restored, and these rooms are best seen from wall-walk level.

The Well 🔟 and Middle Gate 🔟

As the path leads downhill towards the far end of the outer ward, look out for several triangular stones in the pavement edge. These are coping stones, perhaps from a crenellated parapet to the great hall range. They were set here during restoration works in the second half of the twentieth century.

The path ends in one of the most complex areas of the castle, the division between the outer and inner wards. Because the inner ward contained the royal apartments, it could be sealed off from the outer courtyard and defended separately if necessary.

The natural rock was quarried away to create a dry ditch. It was originally bounded to the west by the gables of the kitchen and great hall ranges, with a solid causeway between them crossing the ditch. On the right-hand side of the causeway stood the castle's well. On the opposite side of the ditch rose the massive stone expanse of the cross-wall that separated and defined the two parts of the castle. This wall contains a single small door, now called the middle gate. It was given additional protection by a small guard-house or turret on the outer ward side, and could be completely secured by raising a drawbridge that ran parallel with the face of the cross wall to rest on the far end of the causeway, as shown in the reconstruction drawing.

The original layout is hard to visualize today because some features have disappeared, such as the drawbridge house and the drawbridge itself. Although in need of repair by the mid-fourteenth century, the wooden bridge was still a feature in the 1520s, when Dafydd ap Tudur Llwyd and his servant received 2s. 4d. for 'makyng anewe brigge to entre into the ynder (inner) warde of the said castell'. This was to be the last replacement of the bridge, which evidently needed repairs almost at once. In 1532, labourers began to fill the gap with rubble so that the causeway led all the way to the middle gate. This is the arrangement that we see today. The sloping edge of the pit, however, is still visible in the masonry on the east face of the well.

The castle's well is 91 feet (27.7m) deep, and fed by a spring and water filtering through the rock from the ground surface above. In the original design, the well rose incongruously from the bottom of the rock-cut ditch with freestanding masonry on two sides. In 1525, an account includes slates for two pitches of a roof-covering over the well, one batch of which had not been delivered from Ogwen in northern Snowdonia at the time of the account. In the generally critical survey of the castle in 1627, the well received the favourable comment 'water enough and singuler good'.

A reconstruction drawing showing how the arrangement of the well and drawbridge to the middle gate may have worked in the late thirteenth century (Illustration by Chris Jones-Jenkins, 2005).

Although roofless and lacking floors, the royal apartments in the inner ward are the best-preserved suite of medieval private royal chambers in England and Wales.

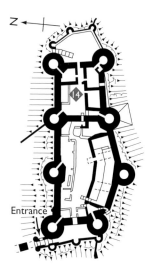

The Inner Ward ◆14

Beyond the causeway, the middle gate leads through the cross wall into the eastern part of the castle, the inner ward. It was here that between 1284 and 1286, the master mason, James of St George, the master carpenter, Henry of Oxford, and the engineer, Richard of Chester, built a suite of apartments for Edward I and his queen, Eleanor of Castile (d. 1290). The inner ward was a private enclosure for the most important members of the royal household, and contained not only imposing chambers for royal residence and ceremony, but also rooms for the household officers and service rooms for the storage and preparation of food.

The royal apartments stood on the first floor around two sides of an open courtyard. The east range contained one large room; the south

range was divided into two. Timber stairways originally rose from the courtyard to two upper doors: one beside the middle gate and the other directly facing it.

Behind the ranges stood three of the corner towers of the inner ward. Recent research has shown that these towers mostly contained service rooms, rather than chambers of the royal apartments. They were designed with ingenious passages and stairways by which servants and officials could enter the apartments unobtrusively to attend on the king and queen. The main exception to this is the north-east tower, the Chapel Tower, in which Master James built a beautiful chapel for the royal household, complementing the larger chapel adjoining the hall in the outer ward. On the ground floor of the ranges were more service rooms, including the king's kitchen and cellars. The fourth tower, the Stockhouse Tower, contained three storeys of rooms and was the only tower not connected to the royal lodgings. There was also a timber-framed structure built on stone footings on the north side of the courtyard, not directly accessible from the ranges: this may have been the 'granary', mentioned as needing repairs in 1343.

Beyond the inner ward, a postern led out into the royal garden in the east barbican. There was also a path down to a dock on the foreshore, enabling supplies (and visitors) to enter this part of the castle directly from a boat.

The surviving masonry and the thirteenth-century works accounts show that the buildings in the inner ward were erected in several phases. Understandably, Master James was anxious to raise the castle's curtain walls and towers first, and the residential buildings were only begun in 1284/85 when these defences were well under way. Though it was always the intention that the towers should communicate with the apartments, the layout of the rooms had evidently not been fully designed, and there are several places where the later floors and cross walls sat awkwardly with earlier windows in the curtain wall.

Though parts of royal apartments from this period survive at other castles in Wales and England, including Caernarfon, Harlech, Leeds (Kent) and the Tower of London, the buildings at Conwy are by far the most complete. Despite being without roofs and floors, they are otherwise little altered from their original design.

As well as their exceptional state of preservation, they are also well documented in most periods from their initial construction through to their decline and abandonment in the mid-seventeenth century. They provide a unique source of information for the changing modes of life in the English royal court. They show that from an original layout with two separate entrances, probably serving the chambers of Edward I and Queen Eleanor, the apartments were later converted into a single unit. Documents of the sixteenth and seventeenth century show that at this time it was entered only through the eastern side. The rooms became progressively more private as the visitor passed through them in a clockwise direction; in the

sixteenth century they were known as 'hall/great chamber', 'outer chamber' and 'inner chamber', while in 1627, the terms were 'great chamber', 'presence chamber' and 'privy chamber'.

Lying far from the centre of court activity in the south-east of England, the royal apartments at Conwy were rarely used for their intended purpose. The 1284/85 accounts mention 'the king's and queen's chambers', but Eleanor of Castile died in 1290, having spent several years in Gascony, and can only have visited Conwy as a building site in 1284: certainly 'queen's chamber' is not mentioned in any later documents. Edward himself was forced to shelter here over Christmas 1294 and early 1295 (p. 10). In April and May 1301, the future Edward II stayed at Conwy to receive homage as prince of Wales. Finally, an eyewitness account of the events of August 1399, leading up to the deposition of Richard II, describes and depicts several tense scenes in these apartments while the king was in residence. These are the only known occasions when the apartments actually housed the king and his court.

Impressive apartments survive in the gatehouse at Harlech Castle, also built for King Edward I, but they are not as complete as those preserved in the inner ward of Conwy.

The royal apartments at Conwy were rarely put to their intended purpose of housing the king and queen. Edward I stayed here over Christmas 1294 and early into 1295; his son, the future Edward II, also stayed at Conwy in 1301 to receive homage as prince of Wales. In this manuscript illustration, Prince Edward is created prince of Wales by his father, King Edward I (British Library, Cotton Ms. Nero D. II, f. 191v).

The king's great chamber
overlooks the courtyard to
the left of this picture. The
first-floor doorway was
reached by a timber stair.

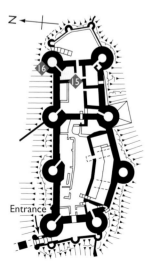

The Royal Apartments

The tour will describe the various parts of the royal apartments together with the ground-floor and tower rooms that served them. The main rooms can most easily be seen from the ground floor, but the passages and stairs, which gave access to these rooms from the towers, mostly remain open. The stairs also lead to the wall-walks and the tops of the towers, from where the whole complex can be seen at a glance.

King's Great Chamber 15

The largest room in the inner ward was the king's great chamber. It occupied the first floor of the east range and was originally entered by a roofed timber stair, probably the 'oriel in the middle of the castle' built in 1286 by Master Henry of Oxford. Here, the monarch would receive visitors, work and occasionally dine in private away from the other occupants of the

castle. This room can be seen from ground level by passing through the arch directly opposite the middle gate and turning left. The term 'great chamber' was used in documents of the sixteenth and seventeenth centuries and may well have been its original name, though occasionally, as in Henry VIII's reign, the room was also confusingly known as a hall.

The great chamber contains a large fireplace in its west wall, beside an elaborate window with 'St Andrew's Cross' tracery. This window, larger than the others in the royal apartments, is an original feature of the 1280s. The design of its tracery is extraordinarily progressive for its time and was once thought to be an insertion of the 1340s. However, the 1340s did see an important alteration in this room: the replacement of the original timber roof structure with stone arches, similar to those inserted in the great hall range in the outer ward. In the great chamber and other parts of the royal apartments, the springers for several of these arches can be seen on one side only of the room; either they were never completed, or some of the evidence for their existence was removed during later restorations. Three large windows overlooked the garden in the barbican, with the river beyond.

The ground-floor room under the great chamber was described in 1627 as 'a large arched room used for a cellar'. Though provided with a fireplace, this room was originally used as a store, for which it was ideally situated, close to the entrance from the dock and adjacent to a private stair leading up to the first-floor apartments. At the north-east corner, the cellar also gave access to the ground floor of the Chapel Tower, a room that now contains an exhibition, but was originally another cellar.

Chapel 16

Leaving the cellar and turning left brings the visitor to the east gate-passage, from which stone stairs rise to either side within the thickness of the east curtain wall. That on the left runs northwards to the Chapel Tower. The stair passes a damaged opening on the left that led directly into the great chamber. Further up, where the passage becomes level, another stair on the right descends inside the curved wall of the Chapel Tower to its cellar and a goods entrance, into which supplies could be hoisted from the path below. These two stairs, and a spiral stair to the upper levels of the tower, meet at the door into the chapel.

The chapel is the most beautiful and atmospheric room in the castle, particularly since 1966, when the tower's roof and floors were recreated. The chapel served the apartments in the inner ward as a more private counterpart to that in the outer ward. During royal visits, the travelling clerics of the royal household would have officiated here, rather than the castle's own chaplain. It remained in sporadic use at least until the sixteenth century; in 1533, Bishop Doffe was paid for 'halowyng the aulter in the castell', presumably because services had lapsed. In 1627, this was one of the few rooms in any of the towers into which one could go safely, though later in the century it was

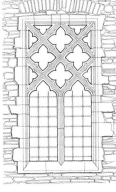

The courtyard-facing window of the king's great chamber as it appears today and a reconstruction of its 'St Andrew's Cross' tracery (Chris Jones-Jenkins, after Toy 1936).

The courtyard-facing window of the queen's chamber as it appears today and a reconstruction of its tracery (Chris Jones-Jenkins, after Toy 1936).

During the events that led to his abdication in 1399, King Richard II stayed at Conwy. On the altar in the royal chapel, Henry Percy, the earl of Northumberland (d. 1408), swore an oath of no treachery to the king. In this early fifteenth-century depiction of the scene, the king wears a black hood (British Library, Harley Ms. 1319, f. 41v).

reduced to ruin. Antiquarian visitors thereafter interpreted the chapel either as part of the king's chamber, as the queen's chapel or as 'Queen Elinor's Toilet'. The association of this tower with Eleanor of Castile, which remained into the twentieth century, has no historical basis.

The chapel is a circular room, illuminated by slit windows on the north and south sides and by three larger lancet windows in the vaulted eastern recess that formed the chancel, where the priest celebrated Mass. The chancel also contains weathered remains of decorative blind arcading around the lower walls in the form of seven trefoil-headed niches. The niches contained seats — sedilia — for the priests. The arcading formerly projected slightly into the body of the chapel and supported a wooden beam bearing a Crucifix, conceivably the 'image' bought for the chapel in 1286. Flanking the chancel were two smaller rooms. One probably served as a vestry, which was used to house the vestments; two locks were bought for its door in 1535. The other room would have been a sacristy, where the sacred vessels were stored in safety.

Following common practice in medieval royal palaces, the chapel communicated directly with the king's great chamber. Lying behind the chapel was also a small guardroom or waiting room, which contained a latrine for the great chamber. In 1627 this guardroom was used as a buttery for dispensing wine. A narrow passage led from this room to the great chamber door.

Climbing up the spiral stair outside the chapel door, you reach one of the most interesting features to be found in any surviving medieval castle chapel complex. It is a 'watching chamber' designed so that King Edward or Queen Eleanor could observe in private services in the chapel below. Such arrangements prefigure similar private watching chambers, known as 'holy-day closets', attached to domestic chapels in late medieval and Tudor houses and palaces. Similar rooms can be seen flanking the chapel at Beaumaris Castle. At Conwy, the watching chamber was even provided with its own latrine. Still higher, the

room above the chapel contains a large fireplace and an impressive two-light window. It is more domestic in character and may have served as accommodation for the chaplain.

The King's Tower 17

Returning down the main stair brings the visitor again to the east gate-passage. On its south side, another stone stair rises twelve steps through the curtain wall, mirroring the stair to the chapel. This passage led into the King's Tower and the range of the royal apartments running along the south side of the courtyard.

Known since at least the nineteenth century as the King's Tower, it has often been claimed that it housed Edward I's inner chambers. More recent examination of the building, however, together with later repair accounts, suggests that this corner was a 'backstage' area with rooms for the most important officers of the household in the tower and a kitchen adjoining it at ground-floor level in the south range.

A cutaway reconstruction of the Chapel Tower as it may have appeared at the end of the thirteenth century. The king himself could hear the services in the royal chapel from a small watching chamber above (Illustration by Chris Jones-Jenkins, 1991).

Opposite: The chancel of the little royal chapel, with its beautiful stone-vaulted roof and three lancet windows. The small rooms to either side probably served as a vestry and a sacristy — for the safe keeping of the vestments and sacred vessels used during the services.

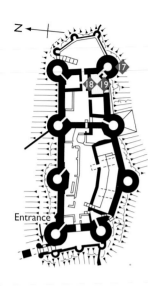

A cutaway reconstruction of the King's Tower, kitchen and king's chamber in the late thirteenth century. This drawing reveals the various narrow passageways that connected the kitchen and service rooms in the King's Tower with the king's chamber on the first floor of the royal apartments. This is the room where the monarch spent much of his day and slept at night (Illustration by Chris Jones-Jenkins, 2007).

The rooms in the tower were linked to each other by a spiral stair and only communicated with the main apartments by narrow and dark passages. They are therefore more likely to have accommodated servants and household officers than the king or queen. The ground-floor room, adjacent to the kitchen, would have been ideal for the treasurer or comptroller who checked goods passing into and out of the kitchen. His room lay over a basement, which can only have been reached by ladder from inside the room itself, potentially a strongroom for money or valuables. The first-floor room would have suited another important official such as the steward, with a large two-light window overlooking the entrance from the dock, though like the ground-floor room, its fireplace was simpler in design than many in the castle. It was served by a latrine, reached by a short passage and antechamber, in the south curtain wall. In contrast, the highest room in the tower was not heated and would have been most appropriate for the king's squires or pages.

King's Kitchen 18

Returning to the cross passage at the bottom of the tower, five steps lead down to the ground-floor chamber of the south range. This room is identified in the 1627 survey as the kitchen. It had also served as such in the thirteenth century, when it was specifically the private kitchen for the king. It is notable that the fireplace in its west wall was one of the largest in the castle, entirely suitable for preparing the king's food, while the door in the south wall to the left of the fireplace was built for clearing waste onto the rocks below. Also on the south wall, to the left of this door, two horizontal lines of shallow marks indicate where a wooden dresser and an upper shelf were fixed to the wall, perhaps in the 1530s when several repairs were carried out to the kitchen.

The King's Chamber 19

On the first floor over the kitchen lay a rectangular room interpreted as Edward I's own chamber. Here, the king would spend much of his time during the day and sleep at night. This room,

with a fireplace and a latrine reached through the side of a window in the south curtain wall, could be entered both from the great chamber and from the queen's chamber to the west. By the sixteenth century, the pattern of circulation around the apartment had changed, and this had become the second room ('outer chamber') in a one-way sequence of increasingly private spaces, starting with the great chamber and ending in an 'inner chamber' to the west. This plan remained in 1627, when the room was known as the 'Presence Chamber', the room in which the king's throne stood under a canopy of state, and where audiences would have been held.

Once again, this room contains springers from the scheme of 1346–47 to insert stone arches to support the roof. In the south wall, scars in the wall plaster show the positions of the original timber trusses. The square sockets, also in the south wall, indicate the medieval floor level. The lower line of sockets probably represents an attempt to strengthen the floor after the original joist ends became rotten, as mentioned in several documents of the sixteenth century.

The castle's designers provided additional discreet access from two floors in the King's Tower, by means of short stairs and narrow passages that emerge in the reveals of two windows in the curtain walls. This complicated design was necessary because the King's Tower contained four floors (unlike the Chapel Tower with three), none of which corresponded to the first-floor level in the main apartment. One passage rises into the south window of the king's chamber: from the kitchen door at ground level, it runs through a small waiting room and past the king's latrine (through a door which could be closed for privacy). The second passage descends through the east wall from the tower's first floor to the eastern window embrasure in the king's chamber. Entry would have involved an awkward climb down from the stone window seat. By these hidden passages, those in the tower could enter the main apartment and attend the monarch when required.

The kitchen for the king was located immediately below his private chamber. This fourteenth-century manuscript illustration shows a cook preparing food (British Library, Additional Ms. 42130, f. 207v).

Although the king and queen's chambers were built for King Edward and Queen Eleanor (d. 1290) — seen here in a fourteenth-century manuscript illustration — the queen had died by the time that the king first stayed in the completed royal apartments in 1294 (British Library, Cotton Nero Ms. D. II, f. 179v).

The dark patch of masonry marks the 1887 repairs to the Bakehouse Tower, which seems to have been deliberately damaged on the orders of the Council of State in 1655.

Queen's Chamber 20

Best viewed from the basement, entered from the courtyard, the final first-floor room in the suite is thought to be the chamber begun in 1284/85 for Queen Eleanor of Castile, but which she never saw completed. Like all the other main rooms, this was provided with a fireplace and latrine. It also contained two large windows overlooking the courtyard, reglazed and fitted with iron bars in 1533, but retaining their thirteenth-century tracery. Eleanor of Castile was an important figure in her own right with a household often numbering 200 people (in addition to over 500 accompanying the king), and in most royal manors and castles, she was allotted a range of buildings of her own. The queen's apartment at Conwy was necessarily more compact than many.

Returning to the courtyard, the visitor can see the original entrance to the queen's chamber: a door at first-floor level in the south-western corner, remodelled, like the window beside it, around 1910. This door, originally reached by an external timber stair, led into a narrow corridor running south to the Bakehouse Tower, now with two doors both turning left into the queen's chamber. However, sixteenth- and seventeenth-century documents show that the plan and function of this corner changed dramatically over time. This first-floor entrance from the courtyard was abandoned, making the queen's chamber the most private area at the end of the sequence of rooms: thus in Henry VIII's reign, it was known as the 'inner chamber' and in 1627 as the 'privy chamber'.

The 1627 survey mentions '2 hansome withdrawinge roomes' at the end of the privy chamber (what was the queen's chamber). The present layout of this first-floor corridor, with two doors leading into it from the privy chamber, suggests that one door served each room. The exact plan of the withdrawing rooms is unclear: either the narrow corridor was partitioned in two, or one of the rooms lay on the first floor of the Bakehouse Tower, which occupies the south-west corner of the inner ward.

Bakehouse Tower 21

The Bakehouse Tower has gone by this name since at least the sixteenth century, on account of the large bread oven built into the wall at ground level. Descriptions of the castle after its abandonment also sometimes call it the 'Broken Tower', because of the enormous fissure in its masonry. This was probably made deliberately in 1655, when the castle was rendered indefensible on the orders of the Council of State, though some later travellers blamed the damage on local people who had made the tower unstable through robbing of the stone. It was repaired with new stone in 1887 at the expense of the London and North Western Railway Company; the extent of the repair can be seen clearly in the tower's interior. Above the bakehouse lay two levels of residential chambers, perhaps originally to house the ladies and officers of the queen.

Stockhouse Tower 22

At the north-west corner of the inner ward stands the Stockhouse Tower, perhaps named after the infamous 'stocks', or foot restraints, that are mentioned in 1519, along with manacles and new locks, for the detention and punishment of criminals at Conwy. The stockhouse was evidently the lowest room, with two residential floors above. Despite this later evidence for imprisonment, the tower was probably built like others for storage and accommodation for the castle's garrison.

East Barbican ◆23
and Water Gate ◆24

Beyond the courtyard, through the east gate-passage, lay the east barbican, an enclosure overlooking the Conwy estuary. From the beginning of the fourteenth century onwards, documents mention a garden here, under the large windows of the great chamber and king's chamber. In the late fourteenth century,

an account mentions vines or trailing plants, while in an early seventeenth-century drawing, it is shown as a formal garden of geometrically planned parterres (ornamental flower beds). The three small round turrets of the barbican wall were described as roofed in an account of 1301: they were probably timber backed. The garden is overlooked, like the west barbican, by elaborate machicolations corbelled out from the wall. These were highly visible from outside the castle, a sign to anyone on the river that the castle was heavily defended.

On the north side, steps ran down beside the Chapel Tower via a gate to the foreshore. At the lower level, a path ran around to the eastern side, where a dock evidently projected into the water, but Thomas Telford's suspension bridge of 1826, Robert Stephenson's tubular railway bridge of 1848 and the 1958 road

The gateway to the inner ward from the east barbican (left) was protected by a row of elaborate machicolations like those in its western counterpart. The windows of the king's great chamber overlooked the lawned garden in the east barbican, which appears in this detail from the bird's-eye view of Conwy of about 1600 (above). The water gate and dock are also shown (By permission of the marquess of Salisbury, Hatfield House, CPM I/62).

bridge have now hidden it completely. On occasion, the monarch or an important visitor could use this water gate to reach the royal apartments without passing through the outer ward of the castle or the town. This arrangement would also allow stores to be brought directly to the castle by boat.

Wall-Walks and Battlements

Six of the towers in both wards of the castle contain restored spiral stairs, giving access to the tower-tops and to the wall-walks, which form a complete circuit of the castle, including the top of the cross wall that separates the two wards. In the original design, gates were fitted at this level against the Stockhouse and Bakehouse Towers, a measure presumably intended not so much for security as for the privacy of the royal apartments. The wall-walk parapets also bear distinct horizontal grooves slightly above the present walkway. These show the position of lead flashing that covered the wall-walks and carried water away from the masonry. These lead roofs were stripped out, like the coverings of the castle's main buildings, when, at the behest of Lord Conway, the castle was finally unroofed and left as a ruin in 1665.

Above: The rebate on the side of the Stockhouse Tower, which marks the position of a gate that could close off the wall-walks between the inner and outer wards.

Above right: The wall-walks on the tops of the curtain walls provided a complete circuit of the castle. This section is looking towards the Prison Tower in the foreground.

The 1742 engraving of Conwy by Samuel and Nathaniel Buck provides some of the best evidence for the form of the water gate at the east end of the castle.

Building Stone at Conwy

Graham Lott, British Geological Survey

The construction of Conwy Castle and town walls required a large and steady supply of both labour and building materials. Wherever possible, most of the building materials would have been sourced locally due to the high cost of transporting heavy and bulky materials in the late thirteenth century.

The Castle

The castle is constructed of three principal stone types. The most common is the local dark blue grey sandstone (formerly known as greywacke sandstone), quarried from the ridge on which the castle and town were built. These local sandstones were quarried from the geological rock unit known as the Conwy Castle Grit Member of Ordovician age (about 440–450 million years). Two contrasting variations of this sandstone were used: the eight round towers are constructed of 'better quality' large sandstone blocks, which are dressed and coursed; the intervening walls use undressed blocks that are thinner and more irregular in size. The rubble wall fill throughout the castle is also of the same local sandstone.

In general, the natural limitations of the local sandstone (soft and laminated) meant that it could not be quarried in blocks large enough to provide suitable freestone for structural, decorative or carved stonework. Consequently, more expensive thickly bedded sandstones were brought in for arrowloops, windows, door jambs and chimneypieces. In the early phase of construction sandstones cropping out across the estuary on the Creuddyn Peninsula were used. These distinctive purple, red or mottled buff sandstones were quarried from the Gloddaeth Purple Sandstone Formation of late Carboniferous age (about 300–315 million

years), and form the principal source of freestone used in all wall openings in the castle, and to a lesser extent in the town walls.

The more sophisticated and finely carved architectural elements of the fourteenth century, notably the roof arches in the great hall range and royal apartments, required better quality freestone. Documentary evidence suggests that the sandstone used in these structures was quarried from the Sherwood Sandstone Group succession of Triassic age (about 200–250 million years). Red and variegated sandstones of this type crop out extensively in the Chester–Wirral area and could be transported relatively easily by sea to the castle. Only remnants of these red brown sandstones now survive, but they present a colourful contrast to the grey sandstones of the castle walls.

The Town Walls

The grey sandstone used for the town walls was largely obtained from the local Conwy Castle Grit Member. However, large blocks of a pale yellow, iron-stained, igneous rock known as rhyolite were used in the town wall and towers along the quayside. Rocks of this type crop out extensively in the Conwy Mountain area, a short distance from the castle, and form part of the Conwy Rhyolite Formation also of Ordovician age.

The upper levels of the north-west tower illustrate the contrast between the dark grey blue sandstone that makes up the bulk of the castle's fabric and the red, purple or mottled buff sandstones used as freestone for arrowloops, windows, door surrounds and other details (Graham Lott).

The use of a pale yellow stone (rhyolite) to heighten the spur wall and nearby towers at the north-east corner of the town walls is particularly clear on Tower 6.

The Town Walls of Conwy

Conwy Castle occupies one corner of a much larger system of fortification, the town walls of Conwy. Running around the historic centre of the town in an almost unbroken circuit of 1,400 yards (1.3km), and enclosing an area of some 22 acres (10ha), the town walls must be considered with the castle as integral parts of a single site raised in one vast construction project. The scale of this undertaking is all the more astonishing when we consider that Edward I's works organization was building Harlech and Caernarfon Castles from scratch at the same time, the latter with a comparable system of urban defences. With three twin-towered gates and twenty-one towers at regular intervals, originally with a ditch around the outside, the town walls of Conwy share many constructional and architectural details with the castle. They constitute one of the best-preserved and most imposing medieval defensive schemes in Europe, an enduring testament to the combined skill and vision of the king and his master mason.

The Medieval Town of Aberconwy

The choice of this location for a new castle and town was by no means accidental. Aberconwy had obvious strategic value in controlling the important crossing of the river Conwy and routes inland. This had been acknowledged by the Normans when they established a castle at Degannwy on the opposite bank and was reinforced by both the Welsh prince, Llywelyn ab Iorwerth, and the English king, Henry III, with their own programmes of additional fortification. However, the place clearly had deeper associations for the Welsh princes. The abbey of Aberconwy, the principal Cistercian monastery in north Wales, had become a major burial site for the Gwynedd dynasty of princes, including Llywelyn ab Iorwerth and his sons, Dafydd and Gruffudd. Prince Llywelyn ap Gruffudd maintained a house close to the abbey (possibly a guest house within its precinct), and it was perhaps in this building that Edward I's emissaries concluded a peace treaty with the prince of Wales in November 1277, bringing the first Welsh war to a close.

The imposition in 1283 of a new English town in a place of such significance to the Welsh represented a violent break with the past, something that would have been apparent within days of Edward I's arrival in mid-March. Some of the earliest changes involved the abbey, whose precinct was immediately requisitioned as the site of a temporary palace for the royal household and as a base for the English administrators; stores and cash were kept in the abbey itself. Edward I petitioned the abbot of Cîteaux (Cote-d'Or, France) for permission to remove the monks to a new site at Maenan, 8 miles (13km) further up the Conwy valley. The abbey church of Aberconwy was soon to be remodelled as the parish church of the new town, served by 'two suitable and honest English chaplains', with a third Welsh chaplain 'because of the difference of language'. But in spite of this last provision, later events showed that the town was almost exclusively for English settlers.

Opposite: Conwy's town walls and castle were built as a single integrated defensive system between 1283 and 1287. This magnificent view from the watchtower — Tower 13 — shows how watchmen could look across the town to the castle.

A number of the Gwynedd dynasty of Welsh princes were buried at Aberconwy Abbey, including Llywelyn ab Iorwerth and his sons, Gruffudd (d. 1244) and Dafydd (d. 1246), seen here in a thirteenth-century manuscript illustration. The removal of the abbey to Maenan, 8 miles (13km) away, allowed the construction of the new town of Conwy (Master and Fellows of Corpus Christi College, Cambridge, Ms. 16, f. 133).

Building the Town Walls

The wide wall-walks of the town wall were created by an ingenious arrangement of multiple corbelling, seen here between the Upper Gate and Tower 14.

The holes to take timber spiral scaffolding are clearly visible on the watchtower (Tower 13); the battlements are also well preserved.

Right: An impression of Conwy as it may have appeared in the early fourteenth century. The former abbey church, in the centre of the town, was retained for parish use and the buildings alongside the castle housed the royal administrators (Illustration by Ivan Lapper, 1990).

The enclosure of the new town with a defensive stone wall was undertaken as part of the same operation as the building of the new castle. Indeed, the details of these works are contained in the same accounts, which sometimes make no distinction between castle and town, referring initially to the town under the heading '*castrum*' (castle). Certainly the works to the castle and town walls were not entered separately in the accounts, and many of the same craftsmen were involved in both. In constructional details, such as the forms of arches and arrowloops, the corbelled-out wall-walks and in the frequent appearance of ramped or spiralling scaffolding 'putlog' holes, there are marked similarities between the walls and towers of the town and those of the castle. The progress of building the town walls is fairly clearly set out in the documents, and other details can be inferred from the standing masonry, which, despite the remarkable uniformity, contains occasional changes that indicate the sequence of building.

Within months if not weeks of the first arrival of the English in Aberconwy, the size and shape of the new town had been determined. On Sunday 16 May 1283, the accounts record payment for a stockade to enclose the site of the town, together with new timber-framed buildings for the royal wardrobe (see p. 63) and a new mill for the king on the Gyffin stream.

Building proceeded in three short episodes. First, during 1284 and 1285, new stone walls were built to protect the vulnerable landward side of the new town. These ran from the edge of the river Conwy at the north-east corner of the town, up the hill (now Town Ditch Road and Mount Pleasant) to the highest point at the watchtower (Tower 13), then southwards towards the Gyffin stream (between Towers 15 and 16), which formerly ran much closer to the town walls than it does today. It is clear

Crossbowmen would have patrolled the town walls. This fourteenth-century manuscript illustration shows a man loading a crossbow (British Library, Additional Ms. 42130, f. 56).

from a combination of physical and documentary evidence that the towers were built first, then the main walling up to wall-walk level, followed by the battlements. These works were finished or nearly complete by the beginning of 1286, when the Frenchman, John Flauner, was recorded as having completed and whitened or daubed the battlements for the northern section of wall. The enclosure of the rest of the circuit — already protected by water — was less urgent. Next, the south wall (to either side of the Mill Gate) was raised under the direction of the Savoyard master mason, John Francis, during 1285 and 1286, and completed by September of that year. During this phase James of St George demolished a building that was in the way, creating a gap between two stretches of wall that Philip of Darley later finished. Finally, in 1287, the circuit was completed with the construction of the eastern stretch of wall along the quayside, though detailed documentation for this work is lacking.

The Design of the Town Walls

Among the most remarkable features of the walls are the regularity of their planning and the uniformity of their construction; only a few minor features indicate any changes of plan during works. Subsequently, the walls have stood the test of time, with only slight alterations made to them since the thirteenth century. For these reasons, the general design is easily described. The walls run wherever possible in straight lines, with D-shaped mural towers set at roughly regular intervals. These gaps are not consistent between different stretches; the east wall along the quayside, probably the last to be built, contains four towers and a gate set approximately 160 feet (45m) apart; 120 feet (35m) is favoured around the rest of the circuit. The towers, apart from the gates and Tower 16, were all roofless and open backed, originally with only a timber platform at the same level as the main wall-walk. Only at this level and on their battlements were

The most vulnerable landward stretches of the town wall, from the quay through to just beyond Tower 15, were built first. This section culminated in the highest point in the circuit of the walls at the watchtower — Tower 13 — seen to the left in this watercolour by Paul Sandby (d. 1809) (The Board of Trustees of the National Museums and Galleries on Merseyside, Walker Art Gallery).

The backs of the towers on the town wall were originally open with the continuity of the wall-walk maintained by simple plank bridges. These could be removed or destroyed in the event of a serious threat developing at any point, so isolating that part of the town wall from its neighbour. Today, modern timber bridges span the backs of the towers.

the towers pierced with openings: thin slits or loops from which crossbowmen could fire either straight out or along the outer face of the wall. As originally built, these were usually simple vertical loops, but in the early years of the fourteenth century, many of them received additional crosses, improving visibility for the crossbowmen inside. The towers themselves and the wall-walks of the intervening stretches of wall were built with crenellations, and, as on the towers on the castle, the merlons contained arrowloops alternating between low and high levels, allowing a field of fire in both the near and middle distance.

An important feature was a system of wooden plank bridges across the open backs of the towers, linking the different sections of stone wall-walk. These were designed to be removed in emergencies so that if an enemy with scaling ladders had climbed onto the wall-walk at any point, the defenders could destroy the bridges to either side and isolate that section. Consequently, beside almost every tower there was a flight of stone stairs from

street level inside the town up to the end of the plank bridge. This arrangement turned each tower and section of wall-walk into a separate unit. Arnold Taylor (p. 19) aptly described the destructible bridges as 'circuit breakers'.

The view from outside the town also displays several details of the construction of the town walls. At many places there are distinct signs of the putlog holes of the builders' ramped scaffolding. Unlike the castle, there is no evidence on the town walls for rendering, but accounts of 1286 include payments for whitening or daubing the battlements of several sections. It may simply be that other payments for whitening the walling below the battlements have been lost, but it is alternatively possible that the relatively thin masonry of the crenellations was alone given extra strengthening by a coating of render. Such a treatment has been identified at San Giorio in Italy, a site in the former county of Savoy from which, as has already been mentioned, many of the leading craftsmen had been recruited for the construction of Edward's castles.

One of the arrowloops modified in the early fourteenth century to improve visibility for the crossbowmen on Conwy's town walls.

Within the Medieval Town

A cast of the earliest known Aberconwy borough seal, probably dating to about 1316 (Society of Antiquaries, London).

Edward I established a number of new towns in Wales, England and Gascony, distinguished by a regular grid of streets around a central market. Montpazier (Dordogne), France, was established as a bastide town by the king in 1285 (Peter Humphries).

Conwy possessed at least three mills, which lay outside the town walls. The mill next to the Gyffin stream was water powered, like that shown in this early fourteenth-century manuscript illustration (British Library, Additional Ms. 42130, f. 181).

The new town of Aberconwy conformed to a pattern, already well established, which has come to be particularly associated with Edward I. In Wales, England and in his lands in Gascony (in France), new settlements were laid out with a regular grid of streets around a central market place, sometimes with fortifications around the perimeter. Such planned towns, known as *bastides*, were occasionally part defensive, but were always more concerned with administration and commerce. Aberconwy, like other towns

established in north Wales by the Crown and English noblemen, conformed well to this pattern.

Early documents give a good idea of the population of the town, where the settlers had come from, and how they were to be administered. The first town charter, issued on 8 September 1284, established Aberconwy as a free borough under the authority of two elected bailiffs and the mayor (who was also the constable of the castle). Trade within the town was to be limited to the members of a gild or hanse, who retained considerable powers to regulate their own activities. Around eleven years later, the earliest surviving list of burgesses (citizens renting land from the king) named 99 people, holding a total of 112 properties, located almost entirely within the area of the walls. Their names indicate that these burgesses were exclusively English settlers, who arrived from many different towns including Faversham, Oxford, Bristol and Nottingham. By the 1300s, a second rental had begun to include Welsh names, such as Einion ap Madog, Maelwyn, and William son of Ioy ap Robyn. However, during this period, there are signs of tension in petitions to the royal council: for example, that 'no Welshman should become a sheriff or royal officer in any commote beside one of the king's castles

quoniam ipse cognouit figmen

in Wales because of the suspicion in which they are held.'

Much of the layout of the medieval town is easy to see inside the walls today, despite several radical changes to the street plan and the construction of the railway through the centre in 1846–47. Three of the modern streets occupy the line of important streets in the medieval town: Berry Street–Castle Street, which runs parallel to the quay and leads to the castle's main entrance; High Street, which climbs into the town from the Lower Gate and quay; and Chapel Street–Upper Gate Street, which also runs uphill and served the Upper Gate, described in the building accounts as 'the gate towards Caernarfon', the main landward entrance to Aberconwy (see plan p. 55).

In the southern part of the walled town, the medieval plan is less easy to trace. Much of the area must have been taken up by the former precinct of the Cistercian abbey, later the parish church and its churchyard. In the south-west corner was the complex of buildings known as the Prince's or Llywelyn's Hall, which may have stood on the site of the Welsh prince's residence. Close by, there were probably other large buildings that served as residences for important royal officers and as the headquarters of the English administrators, including Otto de Grandson, the first justiciar of north Wales. It has also been suggested that the medieval hospital of St John, mentioned as being under construction in an account of 1286, stood towards the southern end of Castle Street, east of St Mary's Church, though no trace of this has survived. A third gate, the Mill Gate, set in the southern stretch of the town wall, gave access to the Gyffin watermill. Two other mills, which were probably horse powered, are also listed as belonging to the burgesses in the early fourteenth century. Apart from the parish church of St Mary, whose western end contains substantial masonry from the abbey church and whose present chancel was probably built soon after the Edwardian

conquest, no buildings of the early town have survived. In April and May 1401, the town and castle were occupied by Welsh insurgents: shortly afterwards, it was stated that 'all the houses in the town of Conwy' had been burnt down. For this reason, the oldest surviving house in the town is Aberconwy House at the junction of Castle Street and High Street. The timber frame of its jettied upper storey has recently been dated by dendrochronology (tree-ring dating) to 1417–18, the first generation of rebuilding after the revolt of Owain Glyn Dŵr. It would be fair to imagine numerous similar buildings, probably with shops at street level and chambers above, along the main streets of the late medieval town.

Aberconwy House, at the junction of Castle Street and High Street in Conwy, was built early in the fifteenth century and represents the first generation of houses constructed after the town was destroyed by rebels in 1401 (© NTPL/Matthew Antrobus).

A Tour of Conwy Town Walls

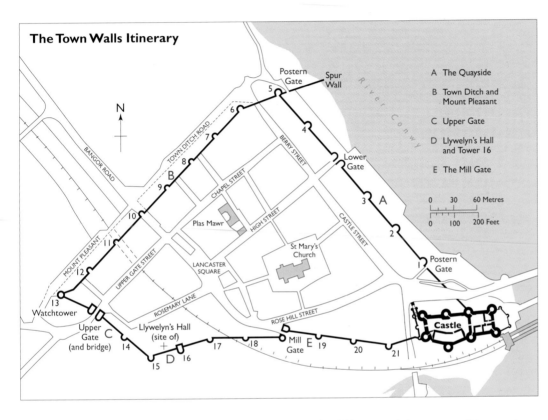

The Town Walls Itinerary

A The Quayside

B Town Ditch and Mount Pleasant

C Upper Gate

D Llywelyn's Hall and Tower 16

E The Mill Gate

Stairs give access to the tops of the town walls between Towers 5 and 17, and the Mill Gate and Tower 21. The town walls have rough stone flooring and no benches. Some sections are steep and can be slippery. Most have handrails.

The town walls are best seen from as many viewpoints as possible and the following tour, which runs anticlockwise around the circuit, is only one of several routes (see map above). Visitors can now walk along the wall-top for a long section, running from Tower 5, at the north-east corner, uphill to the summit at the watchtower (Tower 13), which has excellent views across the town towards the castle and the river beyond. You can then continue downhill, via the Upper Gate, to the south wall as far as Tower 17. At this point the nineteenth-century arch carrying the wall over the railway imposes a break in the wall-walk, but an additional final stretch is open between the Mill Gate and Tower 21.

It should be noted that some of the most interesting features of the town walls can only be seen from ground level, especially on their external faces, and also from within the town, wherever the walls are not hidden by houses and other buildings.

For the best panorama of the town and castle, it is worth leaving the town via the Mill Gate, crossing the car park and taking the public footpath up Benarth Hill. From here, you can appreciate the sheer mass of the castle, its walls and towers rising dramatically from the natural rock in a scene that even the modern construction of the railway and three bridges has done little to diminish.

Opposite: One of the most impressive and imposing views of the town walls at Conwy, looking from the watchtower — Tower 13 — towards Tower 5 on the quay.

The projecting stone near the top of Tower 8 may have been used to suspend a plumb bob to align the adjacent length of town wall during construction.

steep sections requiring footwear with a good grip) towards the watchtower (Tower 13) on Mount Pleasant.

One curious detail of the original construction can be seen at high level in several of the towers on this stretch. On the uphill side of each tower, set well above the level of the wall-walk, a single stone protruded from the surface of the wall. These stones were almost certainly designed so that a plumb bob could be suspended to indicate the line on which the town wall was to be built in the gaps between the towers. They are particularly clear on Towers 5, 8, 10 and 11.

In the stretch of wall between Towers 6 and 7, immediately beside Tower 7, one of the merlons bears a stone finial, similar to the spikes on the castle battlements. Only here and on the south tower of the Mill Gate does evidence survive that the town walls were originally finished in this way.

Towers 10 and 11 bear the marks of nineteenth-century developments in transport. In 1827, a year after the completion of Telford's suspension bridge, the road was driven through the town towards Bangor by the conversion of Tower 10 into a gate. This was done fairly sensitively, with most of the fabric of the medieval tower left in situ around the new opening. Telford did, however, add a largely cosmetic castellated frontage to the outer face of the tower and crowned his new arch with a pastiche medieval parapet, which obscured much of the building's original form. The adjacent tower, Tower 11, shows damage from a hidden source: the railway line from Chester to Holyhead, which runs through a tunnel (begun on 1 March 1845) directly underneath. Subsidence has caused a large fissure and a further crack in the outer face to open up in the masonry. This tower was most recently underpinned in 1963.

The highest point in the defences and in the town is the watchtower (Tower 13), standing on a rocky outcrop. Its setting closely recalls the situation and design of the town walls at Saillon in modern Switzerland (Valais), the former Savoy, where markedly similar open-backed towers and walls run, almost with disregard for the gradient, up the face of an extremely steep hill to the summit. This is not coincidental; John Francis, one of the named master masons responsible for much of the town wall at Conwy, had already had a successful career in his native Savoy in the 1250s and 1260s, including the construction of the tower at

Towers 10 and 11 bear the scars of nineteenth-century development. Tower 10 (above right) was modified to create a new gate through the town walls in 1827. Although Thomas Telford created a pastiche medieval parapet, much of the original masonry was retained. The fissure in Tower 11 (above) appeared after a railway tunnel was dug beneath it in 1845.

Elevation Drawing of the Town Walls (Tower 5 to Tower 13)

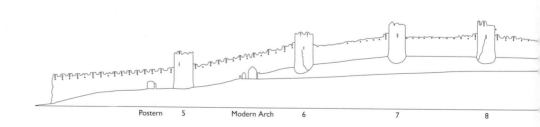

Postern   5   Modern Arch   6   7   8

Saillon in 1261, which still stands today. Such experience gave Francis and his colleagues particular expertise in building over difficult terrain, an ideal preparation for the much larger and more expensive programme begun by Edward I in Wales.

The walls immediately on either side of Tower 13 bow out slightly from their straight course, giving the watchtower a position beyond the line of the walls. A soldier on the tower would have had unobstructed views not along the walls, but over the ditch outside them. To a modern visitor the views all around from the battlements, but particularly back over the rooftops of the town to the castle, are nothing short of breathtaking.

Upper Gate (Towers 13–15)

The Upper Gate is set on slightly lower ground to the south of the watchtower (Tower 13). In the Middle Ages, this was the main landward entrance to the town. Like the Lower Gate, it consisted of two drum towers flanking a central carriageway. The stonework inside the arch shows that the road level has been lowered by several feet from its original thirteenth-century level. Outside the gate, you can see the slight remains of a stone barbican, marked by four small loops, standing on the outer edge of what was the town ditch. The ditch was spanned by a drawbridge, which, when raised, was housed within the rectangular recess visible above the external arch over the carriageway. The gateway

Above: The heavily defended Upper Gate, with the surviving remains of the barbican to the right. This gate was the main landward entry to the town.

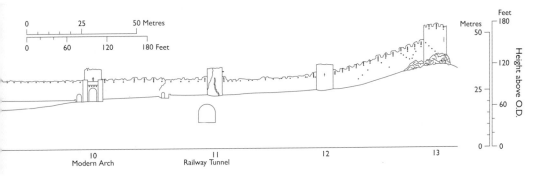

itself was protected by a portcullis and wooden gates, evidence for which survives in the side walls in the form of grooves and drawbar holes.

At a higher level, the configuration of the building is less easy to reconstruct. Most of the rear of the gatehouse was a timber-framed building: in September 1286, the master carpenter, Laurence of Canterbury, received £15 10s. for building a chamber over 'the gate towards Caernarfon'. This type of construction, which also appears at the castle, was fairly common in military buildings; comparable timber-backed gateways existed at other castles in Wales such as Rhuddlan, and also in Edward I's new fortified entrance to the Tower of London, finished only a few years previously. The masonry shows that the drum towers contained floors and roofs. Above the carriageway can be seen the arch in which the portcullis was housed when in the raised position, secured by two wooden beams whose sockets survive in the stonework. The gatekeeper was provided with a small latrine, projecting from the wall-walk at the beginning of the next stretch of the town wall.

The wall now runs steeply downhill. From here you can see how the wall is corbelled out at the top to support the width of the wall-walk. The exterior of this stretch of the town walls is particularly impressive and well worth visiting. At Tower 15, the wall turns sharply eastwards. Since the original course of the Gyffin was much closer to the wall, no ditch was needed on this side.

Llywelyn's Hall and Tower 16

Twenty-seven feet (8m) beyond the corner tower (Tower 15) occurs one of the few significant changes in the masonry anywhere in the circuit — evidence for the phased construction of the town walls. The masonry break is not easily visible today and can most clearly be seen from the fields outside the town. From this angle, the walling to the right of the break is later than that to the left, and was added by the mason, Philip of Darley, in the summer of 1286, together with Tower 16. Philip's task was to fill a gap between two larger sections of the curtain wall, already finished.

Above: The town walls between the watchtower (Tower 13) and Tower 15; some of the best-preserved battlements can be seen on this section of the walls. Note how the ground drops away steeply towards the Gyffin stream.

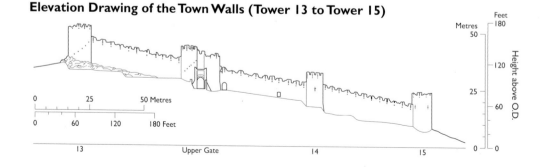

Elevation Drawing of the Town Walls (Tower 13 to Tower 15)

This gap and the misalignment in the walls to either side of Tower 16 provide tantalizing hints of what stood in this area before the creation of the new town.

The wall from Tower 15 ended abruptly at this point almost certainly because an important building stood in its way; indeed, excavations have confirmed that an earlier building stood here. On 7 July 1286, when the whole southern run of the town walls must have been well advanced, Master James of St George was paid 5s. for 'breaking down a certain building that used to be where the town wall is sited,' very possibly in this area. The wall, which Philip of Darley then added to fill the gap, was different in character from the rest of the town walls, containing the only windows in the whole circuit and stone corbels on the inner face to support a roof. This shows either that parts of the old building had survived the 'breaking down' or that it had immediately been rebuilt, with the town wall now serving as its south wall.

As for the identity of this problematic building, its name provides the best clue: 'Llywelyn's Hall'. It seems highly likely that the site, or perhaps a surviving building, was remembered as a place in which the last Welsh prince had lived, and even as the building in which he had concluded the peace treaty with Edward I's envoys in 1277. Possibly Edward I had also used it himself briefly; certainly, when he first reached Aberconwy in the spring of 1283 he occupied an older building in which a chimney needed immediate repairs. In the early fourteenth century, after the investiture of Edward of Caernarfon as prince of Wales in 1301, the rebuilt hall was probably assigned to him. The site was soon further developed with the addition of more land and the construction of a new chapel beside the hall. Unfortunately, neither hall nor chapel now survive. In February 1316, Edward II gave consent for 'our old hall called Llywelyn's Hall' to be dismantled and re-erected inside Caernarfon Castle, where it was used

A reconstruction of how Llywelyn's Hall might have looked; the drawing is based on archaeological evidence recovered from excavations in the area (Illustration by Terry Ball, 1998).

as a storehouse: it has since been demolished again and its exact site lost.

This building sequence had implications for the 'the tower next to Llywelyn's Hall', Tower 16, which stands immediately beside its eastern end. Unlike all the other mural towers, this was a solid building with a shingled roof and a stone back wall. These were alterations made in 1305 to a tower, originally much like all the others, and were designed to convert it into a chamber block serving the hall. Its walls were heightened and three storeys of rooms were created inside it. The first floor was the most comfortable, with windows and a fine fireplace under a stone hood; its walls were squared off to create more space. The tower, sometimes known as Llywelyn's Tower, is the last surviving component of what must have been one of the most impressive residences in the new town.

The only windows in the entire circuit of the town walls lie between Towers 15 and 16; they probably mark the site of a building known as Llywelyn's Hall.

The Mill Gate (Towers 17–21)

The presence of the railway means that the next stretch of wall must be seen from the opposite side of the track, reached from the town through the modern arch. This section of town wall, which includes the Mill Gate between Towers 18 and 19, was built as a single operation during 1285 and 1286, under the direction of John Francis. It is one of the best-preserved sections of the town walls and several parts retain their battlements and arrowloops.

The wall between Towers 17 and 18 was largely rebuilt in 1847 to accommodate a broad arch for the Chester and Holyhead railway. The new walling was designed to blend in with the medieval masonry to either side, with crenellations and arrowloops.

The wall running eastwards from Tower 18 contains a most remarkable feature, without parallel in any other medieval system of town walls: a line of twelve stone projections at high level, corbelled out from the wall. These features, for which an account of September 1286 uses the euphemism 'outside rooms', were individual latrines with outlets originally dropping their waste along the outer face of the wall. The closest parallels are the communal reredorters (latrines) of monastic houses. Indeed, the best explanation for the arrangements at Conwy is that the twelve latrines were constructed as part of a larger building, serving not the apartment of an individual, but an institution. That said, the latrine

Above: The Mill Gate provided access to the royal watermill on the Gyffin stream. Unusually, the two towers do not form a pair; one is round and one is D-shaped. It is this distinction that helps identify the building as the location for the king's wardrobe — an important institution charged with attending to the royal accounts.

Elevation Drawing of the Castle and Town Walls (Tower 15 to the Castle)

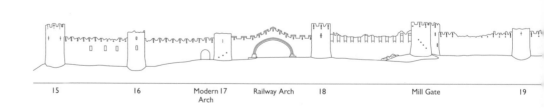

| 15 | 16 | Modern 17 Arch | Railway Arch | 18 | Mill Gate | 19 |

furthest to the right (east), immediately beside the Mill Gate, was built to serve one of the chambers over the gate and was structurally separate from the others. It is to the medieval descriptions of the Mill Gate in works accounts that we need to turn to help identify what other buildings stood in this area and therefore who would have used the latrines.

The Mill Gate, built to give access from the town to the royal watermill on the Gyffin, is tellingly described by other terms in the 1286 account. It is alternatively called 'the towers of the king's wardrobe' or, less directly, 'the south gate and round tower, which is to say the wardrobe of the king's hall'. The 'round tower' is easily identified as the southern of the two drum towers flanking the gate; that to the north is D-shaped. Both towers, unlike those in the other gates in the town wall, contained fireplaces in their upper rooms, which, with the timber-framed chamber that would have occupied the rear of the building, would have been entirely fit for residence or for work. Taken together, all the evidence shows that at least part of the gatehouse, and almost certainly another larger building adjoining it, originally housed 'the king's wardrobe', one of the most important institutions of government in the Middle Ages.

As the name suggests, the wardrobe originated as a branch of the royal household charged with looking after the king's goods, notably his clothes. Particularly over the course of the thirteenth century, the wardrobe's responsibilities were massively extended, and by

the time of Edward I, it had effectively become an entire 'civil service', to use the modern term. Most important in a war or in governing a newly conquered territory, the wardrobe was the institution responsible for keeping the royal armies provisioned with everything they needed, making sure that funds were always ready to hand (supplied to the wardrobe by Edward's Italian bankers, the Riccardi of Lucca), paying craftsmen and buying goods, as well as compiling the accounts themselves. In effect, this was Edward I's logistical corps, and the first fixed centre of its operations in north Wales lay in this part of the town. In the first weeks after the arrival of the English in Aberconwy in 1283, new timber buildings with turf-covered roofs were built for the wardrobe. These probably only served until 1286 when better premises in and beside the Mill Gate were ready.

An account of 1305 mentions 'the lord prince's buildings above the gate at the Mill Gate at Conwy, assigned to the chamberlain as his lodging by the justiciar'. This shows that the rooms had now been reallocated to the chamberlain of north Wales, the officer with particular responsibility for financial administration. Occasional repairs to the building

The remarkable sight of twelve latrines projecting out over the town wall between Tower 18 and the Mill Gate.

Above: Part of a manuscript that records the keeper of the wardrobe's miscellaneous expenses for Conwy in 1283–84 (The National Archives: PRO E 101/351/9).

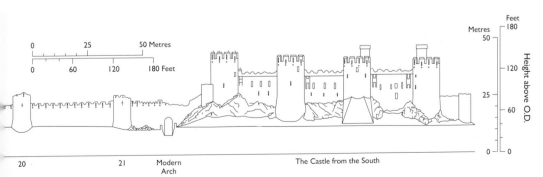

The Castle from the South

In this early fourteenth-century manuscript illustration, a master mason carries the tools of his trade. The recovery of two scribing tools from a building close to the castle may mark the site of the house occupied by James of St George — sometime 'master of the kings's works in Wales' (British Library, Cotton Nero Ms. D I, f. 23v).

were documented until 1401, when it was listed among the buildings destroyed by fire during the rebellion of the spring of that year. Thereafter, no further mention of this function appears in the works accounts and it seems likely that the Mill Gate was no longer occupied for this purpose.

The remaining section of the town wall runs eastward to the edge of the rock-cut ditch, now containing the Llanrwst Road, but in origin a medieval feature dividing the castle from the town. The ditch was closed off by a thin stone wall without a wall-walk. The present wall, running up to the west barbican, probably replaces a drystone wall built in 1286 by Robert Fleming 'in the ditch between the castle and the chamber of Master James of St George'.

It is appropriate to end the tour by reflecting on the possibility that the house of Edward I's celebrated 'master of the king's works in Wales', James of St George, may have stood on the site of the modern car park. An excavation in 1963, close to the edge of the ditch, revealed a large medieval building with timber-framed walls on stone footings. It yielded numerous finds, but most significantly two masons' scribing tools. The site, if uninspiring now, could not be more fitting. It lies in the shadow of the massive fortress that still stands after more than seven centuries, a testament both to Master James's genius as a castle builder and to the implacable ambitions of his royal employer.

Further Reading

Acknowledgements

The author and Cadw would like to thank Peter Brears, Jonathan Coad, John Goodall, Richard Brewer, Ralph Griffiths, Marc Morris and David Robinson for their help in compiling this guidebook.

J. Ashbee, 'The royal apartments in the inner ward at Conwy Castle', *Archaeologia Cambrensis* **153** (2006), 51–73.

R. A. Brown, H. M. Colvin and A. J. Taylor, *The History of the King's Works, volumes 1 and 2. The Middle Ages* (London, 1963).

L. A. S. Butler and D. H. Evans, 'Old Vicarage, Conway: Excavations 1963–64', *Archaeologia Cambrensis* **128** (1979), 40–103.

N. Coldstream, 'Architects, advisers and design at Edward I's castles in Wales', *Architectural History* **46** (2003), 19–36.

O. Creighton and R. Higham, *Medieval Town Walls. An Archaeology and Social History of Urban Defence* (Stroud 2005).

R. R. Davies, *Conquest and Co-existence: Wales 1063–1415* (Oxford 1987); reprinted in paperback as *The Age of Conquest* (Oxford 1991).

R. R. Davies, *The Revolt of Owain Glyn Dŵr* (Oxford 1997).

W. J. Hemp, 'Conway Castle', *Archaeologia Cambrensis* **96** (1941), 163–74.

H. H. Hughes, 'The Edwardian castle and town defences at Conway', *Archaeologia Cambrensis* **93** (1938), 75–92, 212–25.

M. A. Mason, 'Llywelyn's Hall, Conwy', *Caernarvonshire Historical Society Transactions* **56** (1995), 11–35.

J. E. Morris, *The Welsh Wars of Edward I* (Oxford 1901); reprinted (Stroud 1997).

M. Prestwich, *Edward I* (London 1988); new edition (New Haven and London 1997).

D. M. Robinson, *The Cistercians in Wales. Architecture and Archaeology 1130–1540* (London 2006).

Royal Commission on the Ancient and Historical Monuments of Wales, *An Inventory of the Ancient Monuments in Caernarvonshire, volume 1, East* (London 1956).

J. B. Smith, *Llywelyn ap Gruffudd* (Cardiff 1998).

A. J. Taylor, 'The Walls of Conwy', *Archaeologia Cambrensis* **119** (1970), 1–9.

A. J. Taylor, 'The Conwy particulars. Accounts for November 1285–September 1286', *Bulletin of the Board of Celtic Studies* **30** (1982–83), 134–43.

A. J. Taylor, *Studies in Castles and Castle-Building* (London 1985).

A. J. Taylor, 'The dismantling of Conway Castle', *Transactions of the Ancient Monuments Society* **29** (1985), 81–89.

A. J. Taylor, *The Welsh Castles of Edward I* (London and Ronceverte 1986), 45–62.

A. J. Taylor, 'The town and castle of Conwy: preservation and interpretation', *Antiquaries Journal* **75** (1995), 339–63.

A. J. Taylor, *Conwy Castle* (Cardiff 2003).

S. Toy, 'The town and castle of Conway', *Archaeologia* **86** (1937), 163–93.

R. Williams, *The History and Antiquities of the Town of Aberconwy and its Neighbourhood* (Denbigh, 1835), 76–80.

K. Williams-Jones, 'The Taking of Conwy Castle, 1401', *Caernarvonshire Historical Society Transactions* **39** (1978), 7–43.